Wolves
All Over The World

David Instone

Dedicated to
Margaret Bicknell
(1927-2015)
You can shed tears that she is gone or you can smile because she has lived

First published in Great Britain in September, 2015
by Thomas Publications

ISBN 978-0-9550585-8-5

Thomas Publications

Printed and bound by Bell & Bain Limited,
303 Burnfield Road, Thornliebank, Glasgow, G46 7UQ

Contents

Introduction

There have been commendable publications in the past dedicated to recording the dates and scores of the many matches Wolverhampton Wanderers have played abroad, in some cases with scorers and attendances listed as well. Statistics and such 'anorak' content are vital in the right context; indeed, they have been absolutely essential to us in our research over the last few months. However, this project is a little different.

In this book, we do not pretend to have mentioned every game the club have ever played abroad, nor referred to every overseas player in the 'hit or miss' inserts we have included by way of a change of tone. Our focus has been more on capturing the mood, atmosphere and extent of Wolves' travels, with anecdotes liberally sprinkled.

This labour of love has been concerned with accessing new material, in particular countless previously unseen photographs – many of them in colour. They illustrate just how far and how regularly Wolves have exported their talents for the pleasure of foreign audiences. Relatively few of the pictures were taken by 'proper' cameramen or women and we hope there is a postcard-home feel to it because many of the snaps belong to players, officials, supporters and the author himself.

Among those we are therefore grateful to are Tommy Barratt, Taila Miller, Pam and Pete Blakey, Alfred Camilleri, Andy Collins, Per Dyrholm, Ted Farmer, Bobby Gould, Shay Griffiths, Graham Hawkins, Jim Heath, Graham Hughes, John Ireland, Hyder Jawad, Joe from Gibraltar, Stan Journeaux, Ken Knighton, Steve Knowles, Truls Mansson, John McAlle, Neil Morrison, Frank Munro, Phil Painter, Robert Perez, Pat Quirke, Cyril Sidlow, Eddie Stuart, Roy Swinbourne, Bobby Thomson, Terry Wharton, Urban Wigert, Bert Williams, Les Wilson, Martin Wright, plus pro snappers David Bagnall (bagnall.photo@btinternet.com), his son Sam (samphoto@googlemail.com) and Roger Parker, whose excellent work can be found at the www.internationalsportsfotos.com website. And, while we are at it, thanks once more to the diligence of Steve Gordos, himself a prolific author, as an expert proof reader and to another former Express & Star man, Steve Marshall, as a further set of eyes.

Predictably, France was the first overseas country Wolves visited, so that kicks off our journey. The club went there by boat some two and a bit decades on from when the first distress signals were fired from the Titanic. They then travelled to various corners of Eastern

Europe up to the outbreak of World War Two and, as the jet age made the world seem smaller, the club flew to another continent for the first time when going to South Africa in 1951. Our running order is dictated by the sequence in which they went to each country for the first time. Surprisingly, it is 31 years ago since they added a nation to their list.

For the purposes of this book, we refer to 'abroad' as the countries outside England, Scotland, Wales and Northern Ireland. We also tend to give nations the names they were known by at the time of visits rather than what they might since have been called, so readers will see reference to Czechoslovakia, Rhodesia, USSR, East Germany and Yugoslavia in the index and on the later pages. Wolves have played in almost three dozen overseas countries, making more visits to Sweden than to any other foreign land.

They have never been as world-weary as they were in 1972. When Bill McGarry took his players – already fatigued after reaching that season's UEFA Cup final – to America and Canada in the spring, that was only part of it. The squad then cracked on to New Zealand and Australia. Now that's what you call an epic voyage! Not that the manager went the full distance. Half-way through, he decided he had done with travelling for a while and left the Down Under leg in the hands of his faithful no 2 Sammy Chung. But he soon had some wind beneath his wings again – a point he proved by overseeing the shorter hop to Sweden on a pre-season tour only five weeks after his players stepped off their incoming flight from Perth.

A good number of the overseas jaunts have been in competition. It is well acknowledged that those famous floodlit friendlies at Molineux were a catalyst for the launch of the European Cup and the club were in on that from close to the start, too, as well as proving highly entertaining campaigners in the newer competitions such as the UEFA Cup and even the Anglo Italian Cup almost a decade and a half later.

Add all those end-of-season trips, prestige friendlies and pre-season tours and it is very clear we had a rich seam of material to go at when we embarked on this project. We hope and trust that, thanks partly to the technical skills of Liz Instone (eldest daughter of the lady to whom we have dedicated this publication), we are offering fans much that they haven't seen before.

We agree this larger-than-usual book may not be ideal for the beach on holiday. But we hope a good number of supporters who treasure Wolves' worldwide fame and appeal will find a place on their coffee tables for it and see it as a pick-up-and-put down keepsake of those countless trips. Allied with their past successes on the field, this eagerness to spread their wings has brought the club pockets of support in some of the most unexpected places.

Anyway, enough of the preliminaries. Find out your passport and get your bags packed. It's time we were checking in and on our way......

FRANCE

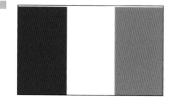

Billy Hartill was in his pomp when Wolves made the short hop to France eight and a half decades ago on their first official overseas tour. As they prepared for what then was no doubt an exciting adventure, Major Frank Buckley's side had just finished fourth behind Everton, Albion and Tottenham – an excellent season's work by the sound of it, until you realise they were immediately followed in the table by Port Vale and Bradford Park Avenue, and the penny drops that it was the Second Division, rather than the First, they were in.

Much as the club came to be feared by foreign opposition, this was a sobering two-match welcome to the world of international travel. They lost 3-1 to Spanish club Santander (bottom middle photo) and were overpowered 4-1 in Paris by the Austrian side First Vienna.

The club re-visited France in 1933 as a reward for beating FA Cup winners Everton on the final day of the season to ensure top-flight survival. But the games that followed did little for cross-Channel cordiality.

The clash in Nice was marked by crowd disturbances so serious that Major Buckley led his players off the field, returning only after being reassured by the presence of extra gendarmerie. "I have brought my team here to play football, not to be slaughtered," he was quoted in the Sporting Star as saying.

The game was eventually called off 15 minutes from the end and Wolves' squad

Handshakes and warm smiles before Wolves' friendly in Nice in 1933. But the mood wasn't always as convivial.

are reported to have been carrying a Union Jack and singing 'It's A Long Way To Tipperary' as they walked past a jeering crowd to the station.

Wolves, whose players are seen above relaxing on the beach in Nice (in their braces, of course!), should have faced a team of Czecho-Slovakians, as the Express & Star called them. But a passport hitch befell their opponents and meant they instead took on Vercelli, then one of Italy's top sides. Bristol Rovers were also in the area at the time playing games.

In addition, Wolves visited Racing Club Of Paris, Marseille and Nimes, and relations obviously weren't too strained by the controversial goings-on near the Mediterranean shore-line. Nice visited Molineux the following season for a return fixture.

NCE ET CLUB FRANÇAIS, SON
demi-finales de la belle épreuve internationale,

There was time for one more excursion to France before Hitler and the hostilities brought such travel to a shuddering halt. A game in the capital against the Paris League XI was the penultimate leg of a five-match 1938 tour that also took in Czechoslovakia, Hungary, Poland and Belgium.

As they lost 2-1 to a side strengthened by three South Americans, Major Buckley's team were not helped by having made a 20-hour train journey from Katowice the previous day.

Dicky Dorsett (centre) and Bryn Jones, are thwarted by a defender on one of several pre-war visits Wolves made to France. This game was in Paris, not that you would know it from the skyline.

Surprisingly, until going there this summer, Wolves had been back to France only once since the Second World War – for a clash with Stade Francais in 1948. That game ended in defeat and was part of a three-match European jaunt that also stretched north-east to The Netherlands.

But the next three pages show how France has played a big part both in the national-service careers and international stints of several Wolves players.

Wolves on the attack again in another fixture across the English Channel. A point of interest is the kit worn by the linesman in the background.

Bert Williams and Cyril Sidlow were near neighbours around the time Wolves were heart-breakingly beaten by Cyril's Liverpool in the last-day title decider at Molineux in 1947. While both still at Wolves, they were also famously in opposition at The Hawthorns in the England v Wales Victory international a couple of years earlier and both had good reasons to remember trips to France......

Above: Wolves stars on a servicemen line-up during a visit to the Arc de Triomphe. Jesse Pye is three along from the left, hands at his front, Billy Wright (in the background) is two further along and Cyril Sidlow is at the back, tenth from the left.

WHAT HAVE THE FRENCH DONE FOR US?

Merci beaucoup pour Ludovic Pollet – a big hit.

Serge Romano – miss.

Ronald Zubar – comme ci comme ca.

Jeremie Aliadiere – promising glimpses.

Henri Camara – born in Senegal, groomed in France.....zut alors!

A safe catch by Bert Williams on his full England debut in the 3-1 win over France in Paris in 1949. The keeper, with Billy Wright as support, had also played in wartime internationals. Below: Just two items from his magnificent souvenir collection.

GRAND HOTEL
TERMINUS ST LAZARE
PARIS

THE FOOTBALL ASSOCIATION

CONTINENTAL TOUR, 1949

England v. Sweden
at STOCKHOLM, FRIDAY, 13th MAY

England v. Norway
at OSLO, WEDNESDAY, 18th MAY

England v. Paris
at PARIS, SUNDAY, 22nd MAY

England "B" v. Finland
at HELSINKI, SUNDAY, 15th MAY

In addition to Bert Williams making his England debut in Paris, the city is also where Ron Flowers (with Williams, Billy Wright and Dennis Wilshaw among his team-mates on match day) also won his first senior cap six years later. The wing-half is seen below on his big day.

The proudest of nights for Dean Richards....leading his country out (below) against Brazil in the under-21 Toulon tournament in 1995. Brazil's side contained Middlesbrough star Juninho and Wolves' then record signing was at the helm of a very young team who were managed by Ray Harford and who included, on the other side of the Barnsley keeper David Watson in the picture on the left, the Manchester United pair of Phil Neville and David Beckham.

Dean Richards, whose loan move to Wolves was turned into a permanent £1.5m deal at the start of June, turned 21 in the week of England's stay in the south of France.

Among the press corps in Toulon was Lawrie Madden – one of Richards' predecessors in the heart of Wolves' defence. And Dougie Freedman was in the Scotland squad.

Deano proves Wolves boss Taylor was right

David Instone
reports from France

In association with
Travel Shop Business Travel
Perton, Wolverhampton
Tel: 01902 753030 Fax: 747024

Wolves manager Graham Taylor may have acted just in time — to prevent Dean Richards going the same way as Alan Shearer and Chris Sutton!

The £1.3m centre-half impressively launched his international career here last night with a performance that showed why Taylor was so keen to wrap up the deal before departing on holiday four days ago.

Richards' debut as skipper in the Toulon under-21 tournament might well have put team manager and 'spy-master' Ray Harford on full alert.

And, although Blackburn No. 2 Ray Harford — on his third trip here with the England fledglings — today refused to discuss the performances of individual players, Richards is certain to have been among the 'one or two plusses' he detected

in side's 2-0 defeat against Brazil last night.

Blackburn and Manchester United both monitored Richards's form during his two month on loan at Molineux at the end of the season.

And the player, who celebrates his 21st birthday on Friday, could · have become a firm target for the money-bags Premiership champions, with Harford's club boss Kenny Dalglish rumoured to be arriving in the South of France in the next couple of days.

Richards, now confirmed as captain throughout England's defence of the Toulon title, is tied up with Wolves on a lucrative four-year contract.

While Richards emerges as one of the pillars of the side, Walsall central defender Stuart Ryder can expect to see plenty of action as well.

An already massively depleted England squad — nine players including Villa's Graham Fenton pulled out before the party assembled on Saturday — have suffered further loss.

Dougie Freedman, later of Wolves, made a surprise declaration at the 1995 tournament in Toulon – he said he was happy to stay put at Barnet in the face of Liverpool interest.

CZECHOSLOVAKIA

With war approaching, Wolves line up in Prague. Back row (from left): Bill Morris, Dennis Westcott, George Ashall, Alex Scott, Jack Taylor, Tom Galley. Front: Dicky Dorsett, Bill Parker, Bryn Jones, Joe Gardiner, Teddy Maguire.

It wasn't just Hitler's march through Europe that made Wolves' end-of-season tour of Europe in 1938 an unlikely adventure. The FA initially refused them permission to go.

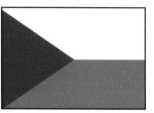

In a letter to the Molineux boss Major Frank Buckley, the domestic game's governing body blocked the trip, which was to include a visit to the Czech capital of Prague, on the grounds that the club had been involved in 'numerous reports of misconduct by players during the previous two seasons.'

Something soon changed in the thinking of the domestic football authorities because, a week and a half after doubts had been expressed, Wolves were setting off on a tour that took in

Belgium, Germany, Hungary, Poland, Austria and France, as well as Czechoslovakia.

A 15-man squad were accompanied by Mr and Mrs Buckley, trainer Jack Davies, masseur Dick Bradford, Express & Star correspondent Nomad and 'ardent supporter' Mr K I Cadwallader.

Prague was the venue for the first of the five games and the visitors caught a cold as they were beaten 4-0 by Sparta-Slavia in front of a 35,000 crowd.

At least Wolves had the consolation of having been put to the sword by a strong side. The hosts included seven of the Czech side who had faced England at White Hart Lane the previous December.

A player's diary in the magnificent Molineux museum, possibly kept by defender Frank Taylor, talks of off-field observations in Prague, such as 'the girls being a little better than in Germany' and: 'Nearly everyone here has got gold teeth.'

Wolves stayed seven miles from the Czech border during the German leg of a four-match pre-season tour in 1996 that also took in Austria.

HUNGARY

Wolves' victory from two goals down against Honved in December of 1954 is considered to be the most famous game in Molineux history. England's nightmare results home and away in the previous few months against the magnificent Magyars – the Hungarian national team – saw to that, with Stan Cullis's men charged with the responsibility of regaining some pride for the country when they then engaged them in battle in a supposed friendly.

They certainly didn't disappoint and victory over Honved was particularly sweet for Billy Wright, who was led every which way when England crashed 6-3 at Wembley and 7-1 away.

Despite the harrowing lessons, Wright struck up a long friendship with his chief tormentor Ferenc Puskas, the chunky and brilliant Budapest-born forward who followed up his four goals in the double-header with Hungary by shining for Honved in their 3-2 defeat at Molineux 61 years ago.

The two embraced warmly when reunited at the redeveloped Molineux in 1993 but what is nothing like as well documented as the epic occasions they shared is the fixture Wolves played against the same club opposition in Budapest in 1963.

Budapest-bound with directors Jim Marshall and John Ireland are (from left) Jim Barron, Alan Hinton, Fred Davies, a hidden Ray Crawford, Fred Goodwin, Peter Broadbent, Terry Wharton, Bobby Thomson, Ron Flowers, Gerry Harris and Dave Woodfield. George Showell, Jimmy Murray and Chris Crowe also went.

BUDAPEST

It wasn't quite a 'return' game as Honved had visited the West Midlands again in the meantime but nostalgia was in the air as a side still under the management of Stan Cullis took off to Hungary in between autumn League fixtures against West Ham and Leicester.

Ron Flowers was the only survivor from the epic floodlit 1954 clash, although George Showell, Gerry Harris and Jimmy Murray had all sampled their fair share of highs against the other European big-hitters.

Showell and Murray travelled in addition to the 11 on duty against West Ham and, at the other end of the experience scale, there was a place in the 14-man squad for what the Express & Star called 'boy keeper' Jim Barron.

The game was the fulfilment of a long-standing promise by Wolves to visit Budapest and a 31,000 crowd were present in the People's Stadium to see Honved take revenge for their famous night-time defeat, the clash in between having been drawn.

Veteran E & S correspondent Phil Morgan called it 'the quietest of games' – one controlled by the home side as they built a comfortable lead with a goal either side of half-time. Ray Crawford pulled one back with a good header late on but the fightback didn't contain any further end product.

Above: Derek Parkin, Sammy Chung and physio Toby Andersen preparing for the 1972 game against Ferencvaros. Below: A much more recent photo of the same Nep Stadium – the venue for England's notorious 7-1 mauling by Hungary in 1954, a month after Wolves secured their first League Championship triumph.

A smallpox outbreak meant many Wolves fans were prevented from travelling to the away leg of the UEFA Cup semi-final in Hungary. In order to schedule the fixture, the club had to put back Easter weekend games at home to Chelsea and away to Nottingham Forest.

HUNGARY FOR MORE?

Gabor Gyepes – a qualified hit.

Denes Rosa – a miss with Mick McCarthy. Others may beg to disagree.

Hungary was also the fifth and last overseas destination during Wolves' long 1971-72 UEFA Cup run. And Bill McGarry's men had to overcome some scares to oust a Ferencvaros side who had reached the semi-final of the competition by including Fenerbahce among their scalps.

Phil Parkes used his feet to save a late Istvan Szoke penalty in the bowl-like Nep Stadium, having also been beaten by the same player from the spot in response to John Richards' early goal. Wolves fell behind to a strike from Hungarian World Cup star Florian Albert but Frank Munro's headed equaliser built on the reprieve given them by their keeper, who then saved a Szoke penalty in their side's narrow win in the return.

Thirty-four years earlier, Wolves had become the first English side since 1909 to visit Budapest and avoid defeat when they drew 0-0 with a Hungarian International XI as part of a pre-war tour of Europe.

Phil Parkes is beaten for once from the spot by the Hungarians of Ferencvaros. The successful taker is Istvan Szoke but the keeper saved a later spot-kick taken by the player in the same game and also kept out his penalty in the second leg at Molineux – as in Budapest with his leg.

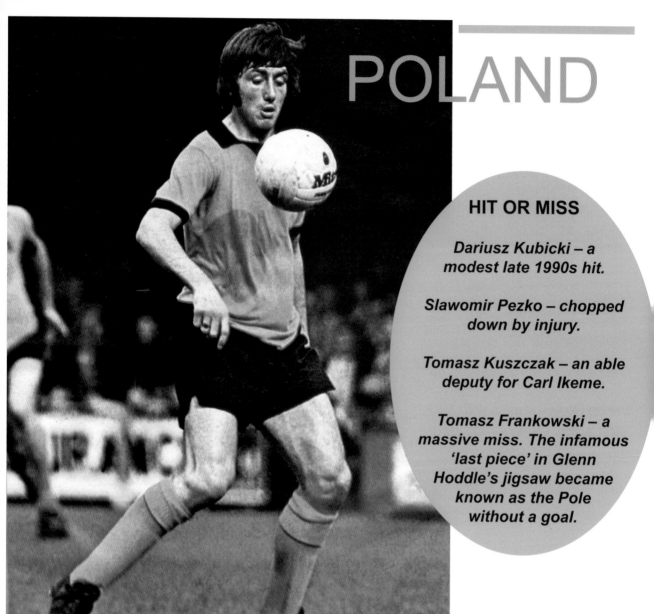

POLAND

HIT OR MISS

Dariusz Kubicki – a modest late 1990s hit.

Slawomir Pezko – chopped down by injury.

Tomasz Kuszczak – an able deputy for Carl Ikeme.

Tomasz Frankowski – a massive miss. The infamous 'last piece' in Glenn Hoddle's jigsaw became known as the Pole without a goal.

John Richards scored his only international goal in Poland – on the three-game East European tour with England under-23s in the summer of 1972 that meant he missed Wolves' trip to Australasia.

Despite breaking his hand in the earlier match against East Germany and becoming stuck in a lift for half an hour with Kevin Keegan and Mike Pejic after arrival in Warsaw, the striker netted the second goal in a 3-0 victory in the Polish capital.

It wasn't his only trip to the country with the Three Lions. He was an unused substitute on the afternoon in 1973 when Bobby Moore equalled Billy Wright's haul of 105 caps in the costly 2-0 World Cup qualifying defeat in Chorzow that ultimately cost Sir Alf Ramsey his job.

Katowice has become a well-trodden path for the England national side. Long before World Cup and European Championships qualifiers, though, Wolves became the first team from this country to play in the city.

On May 18, 1938, watched by 30,000, they twice hit back from two goals down to salvage a thrilling 4-4 draw against Silesia in the third game of their demanding pre-war tour.

Result-wise, the match was a rare highlight for the visitors. They drew two and lost three of their five games – a surprisingly poor record despite the fact they were distinctly unimpressed with the standard of pitches on the Continent.

A book called 'Land of Silesia' was presented to Wolves by their hosts and celebrates an area that falls mostly in Poland but also partly in Germany and the Czech Republic. It is on display in the Molineux Museum, as is a tour itinerary showing that Major Buckley's players arrived in Katowice from Budapest at 6.34pm on May 16 following a train trip that took them through the Carpathian Mountains.

Steve Bull and Andy Mutch toured Switzerland, Norway and Iceland together as members of Dave Sexton's England B squad at the end of Wolves' Third Division title-winning 1988-89 season. Soon after their return, they were side by side against the Poles in an under-21 fixture at Plymouth.

Poland is also the country in which Bully came up with one of the braces he managed in international football. He netted twice in an under-21 game in a 3-1 victory in Jastrzebie-Zdrój in October, 1989, when he had Paul Merson and David Batty among his supporting cast.

Steve Bull and Andy Mutch – more than just a feared combination at club level. They also did some international travelling together.

BELGIUM

You have to be careful how you describe tour fixtures in earshot of ex-players. The suggestion that any game under Stan Cullis was less than competitive is sure to bring disapproving looks.

National pride was always at stake for him even if a match might not have been in either the European Cup or European Cup Winners' Cup.

Nevertheless, all nine of the games Wolves have played in Belgium down the years are officially classed as friendlies, with the northern city of Antwerp figuring prominently among them.

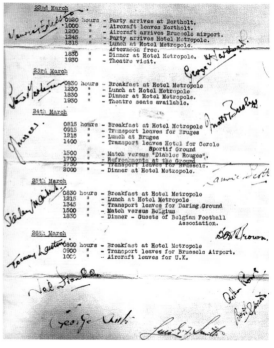

Bert Williams' signed itinerary for a British Forces game against Belgium in Brussels in March, 1945.

The club were first in action there at the end of their 1938 tour when a Combined Antwerp XI beat them 3-1 on the night Tom Galley missed a penalty for the first time in his pro career.

The other side of the Second World War, Wolves were in Antwerp on the first day of November in both 1949 and 1950, the first clash (with Entente Anversoise) being notable for the fact that Billy Wright scored in a 2-1 defeat. The game against Antwerp a year later was drawn.

> **Stan Cullis made a thank-you speech in French after the game in 1949 against a side made up from three local clubs. The gate was more than 40,000.**

Cullis accepted another stern Continental test of his men in the early months of their 1957-58 Division One title-winning campaign when he took them to the Belgian capital Brussels to face Anderlecht in front of a capacity 35,000-plus crowd (photograph left). Again, they came up somewhat short by losing to two early goals, although the fact that they arrived seven hours later than planned because of heavy

Bulletin d'Information du R. S. C. Anderlechtois (Affilié à l' U. N. S. O. C.)
Correspondance : 2, avenue Théo Verbeeck, à Anderlecht.
21ᵉ année - N° 8
Prix : 5

Wolverhampton adversaire de marque

Pour son troisième match en nocturne, contre des équipes étrangères, Anderlecht reçoit aujourd'hui la prestigieuse équipe du Nord de l'Angleterre : Wolverhampton Wanderers Football Club.

Wolverhampton est une équipe de grande classe, la plus prestigieuse peut-être à l'heure actuelle du football britannique, puisque présentement, elle domine nettement tous les clubs de la Ligue, accumulant les succès, se jouant souvent de ses adversaires. Ses références sont multiples; pour s'en convaincre il suffit de jeter un coup d'œil sur son palmarès particulièrement brillant.

Point n'est besoin de longs discours ni d'éloges dithyrambiques pour démontrer la valeur des Wolves.

En Angleterre, comme en France, en Italie comme partout où l'on s'intéresse quelque peu au football, le nom de Wolverhampton est célèbre. Et en Belgique, nul n'est sensé ignorer la loi, dans le monde du football, nul n'est sensé ignorer la grande valeur de Wolverhampton.

C'est cette prestigieuse équipe que le Sporting matchera aujourd'hui; c'est ce team en pleine forme — sur 16 matches disputés cette saison, il en a remporté 11

Mercredi 4 décembre 1957 à 19 h. 30

— que ses hommes trouveront devant eux...

Que feront-ils...? Telle est la question que se posent, depuis l'annonce de la conclusion du match, supporters et sympathisants du Sporting. Répondre à cette question est évidemment chose fort malaisée. En fait, aucun point de comparaison récent n'existe. Ce qu'il est cependant permis d'avancer, et cela avec certitude, c'est que l'on assistera à un très grand match. Tout d'abord, en raison de la valeur in-

OUT OF DARKNESS COMETH LIGHT

Welcome Wolverhampton Wanderers

We are only very happy to have with us today, the visiting team of Wolverhampton, ambassador of the football, but we feel that you accepted to play against R. S. C. Whatever the result may be, this match, people have been can assure you that we are comed here as friends and will also leave us as friends ... Interesting

elle paraît apte à de grandes satisfactions.

Faut-il en conclure que Wolverhampton ? Pas si vite, faut se rendre compte...

fog was a strong mitigating factor in their defence.

The Belgian public might have wondered whether all the hype surrounding Wolves was justified because not even two games there in the month following their crowning as League champions for the second time could bring out the best in them.

After the Anderlecht friendly in 1957, Wolves players were each presented with a timepiece which opened to reveal a team photo of their hosts. The long-time coach to the home club, who were part-timers, was former Blackburn keeper Bill Gormlie.

With the League Championship in the bag for the second time, Wolves' squad and officials are in good heart as they get set for take-off to West Germany, Switzerland and Belgium in the summer of 1958.

At the end of a five-match 1958 European tour which had kicked off with high-scoring wins in Switzerland and Germany, Wolves disappointed yet again in Brussels when competing in a four-team tournament at which local heroes Anderlecht were very much the star attraction.

Wolves lost to Beerschot by the odd goal, then caved in embarrassingly against Juventus to the tune of 5-1, with John Charles scoring one and making two. An excuse was available for the exhausted League champions as Wright, Peter Broadbent, Bill Slater and Eddie Clamp were away at the time at the World Cup finals in Sweden.

Bert Williams had happy memories of Belgium. He went there in March, 1945, with England for a Services international in Brussels, where the reported gate of 45,000 was 15,000 above capacity. "Every time a player took a corner, he disappeared into the crowd for his run," read a match report. The keeper, then still with Walsall, was listed as 955683 Sgt B F Williams and had Matt Busby, Joe Mercer, Frank Swift, Tommy Lawton, Neil Franklin and Cpl Stanley Matthews as team-mates, the squad having also played a game in Bruges the previous day.

For supporters with long memories, there were more 'What is it about Belgium?' laments a decade and a half later when Bill McGarry's team lost in Bruges by the goal – credited to the reluctant Derek Parkin – two days after beating Arsenal 3-1 at Highbury in a fixture to decide the third and fourth places in the 1972-73 FA Cup.

Wolves had hoped to be facing Anderlecht, who arranged a game with Liverpool instead, but the clash with a side who had won the Belgian title by seven points obviously proved more than testing, as illustrated by the heading and scoreline on the Express & Star report of the game below.

HIT OR MISS

Cedric Roussel – miss, an expensive one at that.

Geoffrey Mujangi Bia – went flat in no time.

Jelle Van Damme – bailed out sharpish.

Not so friendly in Bruges as Parkin makes sad error

BRUGES 1, WOLVES 0

Wolves unbeaten record in pre-season friendlies and other games, ended in Belgium last night where an own goal gave the local champions, Bruges, a narrow victory.

The goal came in the fifth minute when Derek Parkin, under no pressure, turned to direct the ball back to Phil Parkes.

But Parkes had left his line to gather the ball and Parkin, not realising he was almost on top of him, diverted it into his own net.

A minute earlier and a powerful Dougan header nearly gave Wolves the lead after good work by Wagstaffe, Hibbitt and Richards, but Sanders, in the Bruges goal, pulled off a fine save.

Bruges turned on the pressure afterwards and Parkes came to Wolves rescue with some brilliant work. He first parried a shot from Lafavre and saved point blank efforts from Lambert and Russman.

In the 30th minute Dougan got in another header which Sanders saved.

BY JOHN DEE

Two Wolves men in the limelight at Bruges last night – JOHN RICHARDS (left) who was booked and DEREK PARKIN whose own goal gave the Belgian side victory.

Another generation, another set of players……Wolves went back to face Royal Antwerp in their first summer under Dave Jones (2001) and had the game in their control with a 2-0 interval lead. But Manchester United's nursery club, who had reached the 1993 European Cup Winners Cup final, hit back to draw and leave their visitors with the record of two draws and six defeats from eight matches in the country.

Antwerpen

Tony Dinning was sent off in the clash, a photo of which is shown below, and Jones hit the roof with his players afterwards, although one of them was content. Costly Cedric Roussel was clearly happy to be back in his home country because this was one of the more impressive games of his easily forgotten Molineux stay, underlined as it was with a goal.

Wolves have made one more visit to Belgium – for a 2-1 victory over Charleroi in July, 2010. The game, at one of England's match venues from Euro 2000, was arranged as part of the deals that brought Adlene Guedioura and Geoffrey Mjangi Bia to Molineux.

23

SWEDEN

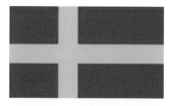

The text-to-photo ratio of this publication is about to undergo something of a change – in this section and certain others, at least.

No foreign country has seen more of Wolverhampton Wanderers than Sweden, so the availability of photographs is substantially increased. This is therefore a much weightier chapter and it's a fair bet that a few pine forests – the staple diet when it comes to scenery in those parts – will be on view over the next few pages.

Jonathan Hayward gently chided me when he said he tired back home while reading my despatches from tours in 1993 and 1994 because they always seemed to be making the point that games were played in picturesque settings at grounds surrounded by woods. Well, see the photo above showing Wolves players watching another game after training in 1971 and also the picture at the bottom of the facing page that captures Geoff Thomas conducting the formalities before a 1993 fixture against Solve, then make up your own mind!

Wolves have had a strong presence in that corner of Scandinavia since the Second World War, particularly in the 1970s and 1990s.

From 1946 to 1999, the club went to Sweden no fewer than 15 times – a statistic that makes it surprising they haven't been at all in the 21st century. So why the popularity?

In Wolves' case, it could well be traced back to the fact that the First Division clash with Sunderland at Molineux in November, 1969 was the one chosen as the first English League fixture ever screened live in Scandinavia.

Hugh Curran's winner on a frost-bound pitch meant the club immediately had a following across the North Sea – one that was cemented by tours in 1971, 1972, 1973, 1975, 1976, 1977 and 1978.

"We seemed to go there every year," said Frank Munro. "If it wasn't for a pre-season tour, it was for games at the end of a season. And sometimes we'd go to Norway in the same summer, a few weeks earlier or later. It felt like a second home to us."

Its relative proximity to Britain, a friendly, largely English-speaking population including many Wolves fans and a climate generally removed from the excesses of the Mediterranean might be seen as attractive selling points of a country the club first visited 69 years ago.

A five-match Swedish tour undertaken barely a year after the end of the war can be accurately viewed as highly ambitious. And it was certainly no stroll in the park for Ted Vizard's side (pictured above). They won two, lost two and drew one of their games.

Hälsning från Malmö

There was also controversy on a tiring excursion that took them from Gothenburg to Sundsvall, Gavle, Djurgarden and Malmo.

In the latter city, Tom Galley was sent off in a 3-1 victory and the visitors' 'motor coach' was stoned by angry local fans. Sorry, perhaps we should have used the words 'usually friendly' supporters on the facing page!

Bert in command

Bert Williams, watched by Billy Crook, catches safely to foil a home forward in Wolves' win in Malmo in 1946. Below: An unflattering editorial suggesting Wolves were an overly robust force in Sweden. Left: One of world football's most stamped and used passports.

PÅ GÅNG
Revolverhampton.

Det renommerade engelska ligalaget | förfogande: mr Gerhar
Wolverhampton Wanderers har vandrat |

Not until 1954 did Wolves return to Sweden, a crushing win over Helsingborg being sandwiched between two victories in Denmark amid the warm after-glow of the League Championship title coming to Molineux for the first time.

The club's name became better known still over there when, in the 1958 World Cup finals, they provided England's entire half-back line in the shape of Bill Slater, skipper Billy Wright and Eddie Clamp, with Ron Flowers at home as back-up.

Wolves didn't go back to Sweden until a new generation of stars, like Dougan, Richards, Hibbitt, Munro and Wagstaffe, had gelled. A three-match visit preceded their successful 1971-72 season and the players are shown being put through their paces on the right by Norwegian-born physio Toby Andersen.

The Doog is leading the way, with John Richards and Les Wilson right behind, followed by Phil Parkes, Derek Parkin, Bernard Shaw, John McAlle, Jim McCalliog and more.

There was silverware at stake when Wolves landed in Sweden in 1972. And they got their hands on the prize by winning the Sir Stanley Rous Cup at the Ullevi Stadium in Gothenburg.

They beat GAIS on penalties 5-4, with Hugh Curran scoring the decisive kick, then defeated Everton 2-1 in a final refereed by Jack Taylor. Gais's goal in the semi was a penalty in normal time and there was the unusual sight of Derek Parkin – a trusted taker for some time before and afterwards – missing his kick in the shoot-out.

Wolves repeated the feat by beating Orgryte and Leicester to lift the same trophy in 1973, the latter as Alan Sunderland netted the only goal of the final.

Frank Munro, player of the 1972 tournament, receives the trophy from Sir Stanley Rous the year after (left), watched by Leicester's players. Above: All the way from Sweden – a cherished present-day player of the year trophy.

With ski slopes as a backdrop, Wolves were preparing for the end-of-tour game against Karlstad in 1971 when the photo on the left was taken. Among the fellow guests at their lake-side hotel were the Rangers squad who were to win the European Cup Winners Cup during a 1971-72 season in which Wolves reached the UEFA Cup final. Bill McGarry's men beat Karlstad 2-1.

Trips to Scandinavia became an annual thing for the rest of the 1970s. Sometimes, there was a visit there at the end of one season and another before the start of the next term.

A 100 per cent win record in 1975 and 1976 was interrupted by defeats in their first two matches of the 1977 trip but they were largely dominant again when they made a popular return visit in 1978.

HIT OR MISS

*Joachim Bjorklund –
utterly insignificant.*

Right: Sammy Chung, Jim McCalliog, Toby Andersen, Phil Parkes and Frank Munro at leisure in Scandinavia.
Below: An understated celebration of a goal by Bobby Gould on the 1976 visit.

A few weeks before Christmas in 1977, Wolves made a quick Swedish visit that has largely disappeared from fans' memories. At a time when the club had won the Daily Express Five-a-Side Championships two years in a row, Sammy Chung took eight players – Richards, Hibbitt, Bradshaw, Eves, Daly, Patching, Black and Kelly – to Norrkoping for a similar tournament played indoors on astro-turf. Three defeats out of three meant they were quickly eliminated.

An extra splash of Gould

Bobby Gould did more than just tour Scandinavia as a player. He took his first steps in coaching over there and consequently put down some of the foundation stones for his long management career. Right: He nets with a diving header against Norrkoping in Wolves' 2-0 defeat in 1977, only to have it unluckily ruled out. Below right: Tracksuit and thoughtful face on....it's time to see things from the other side of the touchline. And below: He's caught in head-scratching pose on the tour of Sweden under Sammy Chung in 1976 – a visit he marked by hitting four goals in the opening game. George Berry is stifling a yawn and skipper Mike Bailey (two along from the far left) stares downwards but Wolves came out of the blocks brilliantly and took the Second Division by storm.

Tours of Sweden became less frequent for Wolves from the start of the 1980s but the winning of promotion in 1982-83 was seen as a good enough reason to get back in the old routine. Cue more forests, fjords and big victories as Graham Hawkins' squad won four and lost one of their five matches over there as preparation for their top-flight comeback.

Although Mark Buckland's late goal brought victory over Norrkoping in a one-game visit to celebrate the 50th anniversary of the Swedish Pools Company in the October of 1984, Wolves didn't head for the country again on tour until a five-match series of triumphs under Graham Turner in 1991 kicked off another round of visits in quick succession.

Swedish Tour Statistics

WEDNESDAY, JULY 21
VAXJO 2 WOLVES 5
Wolves: Stowell (Jones, 46), Ashley (Simkin, 46), Venus, Burke (Keen, 46). Mountfield (Edwards, 46), Blades, Birch, Cook (Thomas, 46), Bull (Mills, 46), Kelly (Roberts, 59), Rankine. *Goals:* Bull (18, 39), Birch (52), Mills (73, 79). *Attendance:* 333.

THURSDAY, JULY 22
NYBRO 1 WOLVES 3
Wolves: Stowell, Ashley, Edwards, Burke, Mountfield, Blades (Venus, 46), Keen, Cook, Bull, Kelly, Thomas. *Sub:* Mills. *Goals:* Burke (34), Kelly (82), Bull (84). *Attendance:* 1,004.

SUNDAY, JULY 25
LJUNGBY 0 WOLVES 3
(abandoned after 82 minutes because of injury to Ljungby's Peo Andersson).
Wolves: Jones, Simkin, Edwards, Rankine, Mountfield (Ashley, 46), Blades (Venus, 51), Birch, Thomas (Cook, 46), Mills (Bull, 46), Kelly (Roberts, 46), Keen (Burke, 46). *Goals:* Mills (30, 44), Birch (32). *Attendance:* 250.

MONDAY, JULY 26
SAXEMARA 1 WOLVES 3
(AT RONNEBY)
Wolves: Stowell, Simkin (Ashley, 69), Venus, Burke, Mountfield, Blades, Keen, (Birch, 46), Cook, Bull, Kelly, Thomas. Sub: Mills. *Goals:* Bull (29), Thomas (59), Kelly (65). *Attendance:* 1,557.

WEDNESDAY, JULY 28
VALDERMARSVIK 1
WOLVES 8
Wolves: Jones, Ashley, Edwards, Rankine, Mountfield, Simkin (Blades, 22), Birch, Cook (Thomas, 31), Bull (Mills, 46), Roberts, Burke (Venus, 15). *Goals:* Roberts (14, 64, 90), Mountfield (17), Cook (22), Edwards (56, 73), Mills (82). *Attendance:* 500.

APPEARANCES: Stowell 3, Jones 3, Ashley 5, Simkin 4, Edwards 4, Venus 5, Burke 5, Rankine 3, Mountfield 5, Blades 5, Birch 4, Keen 4, Thomas 5, Cook 5, Bull 5, Kelly 4, Roberts 3, Mills 3.
GOALS: 22 (Mills 5, Bull 4, Roberts 3, Birch 2, Edwards 2, Kelly 2, Burke 1, Thomas 1, Mountfield 1, Cook 1).

Following that goal-laden jaunt, interest was high two years later when Wolves returned to Sweden, the summer signings of Kevin Keen, David Kelly and new skipper Geoff Thomas having raised the club's profile considerably and boosted their promotion ambitions.

The win in Nybro is captured above while the vital stats, as used back home in the programme, appear on the left.

Fury over Ashley's Swedish sickener

By David Instone in Sweden

Wolves' pre-season tour to Sweden erupted in fury last night when defender Kevin Ashley was sent off for a tackle that broke an opponent's leg.

Ashley's lunge at 30-year-old Per Andersson left the midfielder with the third division team Ljungby nursing an agonising two fractures at the front and side of the shin.

Billy Wright, who showed his willingness to muck in by occasionally acting as ball-boy during training on tour, receives a gift on behalf of the club before the 1993 game against Saxemara.

'Old-Timer' David Kelly, Lee (Freddie or Larrie) Mills and Karen's hero Geoff Thomas

Above left: Geoff Thomas with the captain of Nybro and the match officials. *Below left:* Geoff exchanges pennants with the Ljungby skipper. *Below right:* The picturesque Nybro ground.

Images of 1993 life on tour. Above: The Ljungby v Wolves clash that was ended eight minutes early by a serious injury – and some grim headlines for Kevin Ashley. Left: How the author's photographs were used in the club programme for the first home match of the following season.

Vaxjo, a venue for Wolves in 1993, was the birthplace of 2004 free signing Joachim Bjorklund in 1971.

SWEDEN

Wolves had an unusual experience on tour in 1994 – they played in different countries on successive nights, following up a win over Hvidovre in Denmark by thrashing Solve (above) after they had settled into their hotel in southern Sweden (right). The hectic schedule might explain why they were in change colours for the second assignment.

Goals came in rich supply on the 11-day trip and eight rained in during a Saturday afternoon romp against Smedby, in which Mark Rankine is seen on the ball in the photo on the right.

Det aktiva hotellet!
Hotell Hanöhus

A 2-0 victory over Kristianstad kept Wolves on the winning trail on their sun-drenched travels 21 summers ago, with a red-shirted Graham Taylor, no 6 Steve Harrison and the rest of the staff looking on. And a 100 per cent record was assured by the victory over Asarum that was built on a Lee Mills hat-trick. With Geoff Thomas in a fitness battle, Peter Shirtliff was captain and exchanged pennants with his Asarum counterpart (below).

THE FUTURE'S GOLD

We didn't know it at the time but there was a strong (future) Wolves connection at the 1992 European Championships finals in Sweden. Although Steve Bull wasn't present, England's manager was Graham Taylor and his unsuccessful squad contained Keith Curle, Tony Daley and Andy Sinton, all of them destined to move to Molineux later in the 1990s.

For the best part of two decades, it was as if the club had had a Swedish timeshare week or two but new destinations started to appear on their map in the second half of the 1990s and only one more Swedish visit has followed – under the management of Colin Lee in 1999.

Maybe it was the sad memory of Steve Bull announcing his retirement on the steps of a hotel in Solvesborg that prompted the broadening of horizons. Wolves, for well over a decade and a half, were done with a country that had become almost a happy second home.

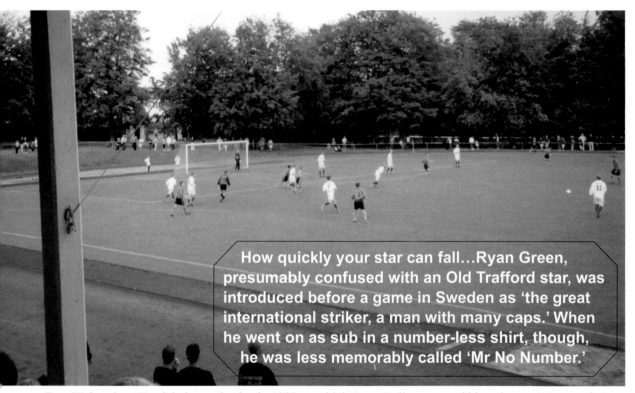

How quickly your star can fall...Ryan Green, presumably confused with an Old Trafford star, was introduced before a game in Sweden as 'the great international striker, a man with many caps.' When he went on as sub in a number-less shirt, though, he was less memorably called 'Mr No Number.'

Top: Wolves beat Hassleholm on the day in 1999 on which Steve Bull announced his retirement. Lower photo: Another win in southern Sweden three days later – this time against Solve, who provided the side's tour base.

Sölvesborg

The pre-season tour of 1999 was effectively a farewell to two hugely popular forwards. Not only did Steve Bull finally admit defeat in the face of chronic knee problems but Robbie Keane was in the room marked 'departures' ahead of his move to Coventry less than a fortnight into the new season. A third goal-scoring great, John Richards, by then the club's MD, is pictured in the middle of the back row below, just to Bully's left.

HOLLAND

Sir Jack Hayward made a point of saying in 1994 that he welcomed the signing of John de Wolf because the Dutch had been good allies behind the home effort during the war.

A trip there in 1948 didn't therefore entail the sensitivities that other destinations might have done and Wolves made themselves at home with odd-goal victories in Rotterdam and Amsterdam within a couple of weeks of finishing fifth in the top flight. Stan Cullis's side also played in France on the same trip.

The attendances on the tour are worth a mention. There were 60,000 at the game against a Combined Dutch XI containing six full internationals while 50,000 saw Jesse Pye net the only goal against Holland's National Association side.

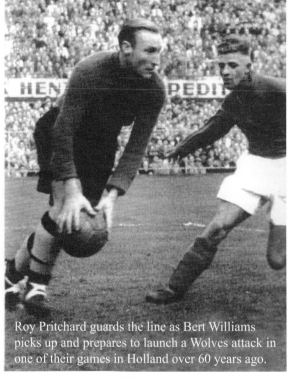

Roy Pritchard guards the line as Bert Williams picks up and prepares to launch a Wolves attack in one of their games in Holland over 60 years ago.

John de Wolf, a huge figure with Feyenoord and Holland before being brought to Molineux by Graham Taylor, made a sizeable imprint over here, too. At Port Vale in 1995, he became the first Wolves defender for 92 years to score a hat-trick.

Roy Swinbourne watches a cross from Peter Broadbent float in during Wolves' 2-2 draw with a Dutch XI in Rotterdam in October, 1952.

Wolves returned to the Netherlands in October of 1952 and played a Dutch XI in front of 52,000 in Rotterdam as Holland assembled some of their top players for what they saw as vital preparation for a 'derby' fixture against Belgium the following week.

Billy Wright's first appearance in the country was marked by an early penalty miss from Leslie Smith but the same player came up with Wolves' first goal and the second was a somewhat fortunate effort from Peter Broadbent, only for the hosts to hit back for a 2-2 draw.

Frank Munro had good reason to remember the 1970 trip to the Netherlands during a pre-season tour centred mainly in West Germany.

He stepped forward as an emergency goalkeeper for the early-August friendly against Groningen after Phil Parkes had been taken ill on a flight and rushed to hospital for an appendix operation. John Oldfield was on the trip but had a foot problem and plans to fly Rod Arnold out had to be scrapped when the third-choice man suffered an injury of his own in training back at the racecourse.

Groningen declined Wolves' appeal to borrow a keeper for the day and duly won 1-0, although Munro performed impressively after immediately volunteering for duty. He was beaten only by a first-half penalty that he himself had conceded.

A victory in the Netherlands came early in Wolves' goal-filled run to the UEFA Cup final in 1971-72, their 3-1 success against Den Haag being built on strikes by Jimmy McCalliog, Derek Dougan and substitute Kenny Hibbitt, all in the final half-hour. McCalliog celebrates his goal below, with Dougan and Dave Wagstaffe (far right) also in the picture.

Den Haag had their own 'Peter Knowles' in left-back Korecvaar, who, as a Jehovah's Witness, said he would play for the Kingdom of God but not the Kingdom of Holland. Also in the Dutch side in 1971 against Wolves was Dick Advocaat – appointed in March, 2015 as Sunderland manager.

Den Haag's Zuider Park ground had been a dangerous place to be 30 years before Wolves visited it at the second stage of their exciting UEFA Cup adventure. One allied pilot, returning home from a raid over Germany, urgently needed to dump some of his unused load to save fuel and managed to leave a bomb buried in a park next to the stadium.

A 17,000 crowd were in place in 1971, when the hosts were wearing an unusual kit of green shirts, red shorts and yellow socks.

Now then, you two, let's make it a good clean fight...

Sparks flew as well when Wolves faced the same Dutch club in the 1967 American tournament. Rival captains Derek Dougan (clad in his club's all white change strip) and Piet de Zoete are seen above at the pre-match formalities – and no wonder the American referee looks a bit tense. At the first of the two meetings of the clubs in the States, in San Francisco, Ernie Hunt, The Doog and an opponent were sent off and wingers Dave Wagstaffe and Paddy Buckley were carried off, with Waggy ending up in hospital.

As if that trail of havoc wasn't enough, Les Wilson had a water bucket emptied over his head by a Dutch official.

HIT OR MISS

John de Wolf – certainly made an impression.

Rajiv van la Parra – a big hit of the future, we hope.

Hans Segers – had his moments, especially an FA Cup penalty save at Leeds.

Stefan Postma – did an okay job.

Robin van der Laan – no real impact.

In May, 1970, a day after the seniors flew out on an Anglo Italian trip, a young Wolves side departed for a tournament in Breda, southern Holland. The squad underlined the emerging talent, with Barry Powell, Rod Arnold, Jimmy McVeigh, Peter Eastoe, Steve Daley, Alan Sunderland and Kenny Hibbitt all included.

It was a different story on the European combat front when Wolves made another short hop over the North Sea in the after-glow of their second League Cup conquest. John Barnwell's side were beaten 3-1 in Eindhoven in the first leg of their opening UEFA Cup assignment and were left rueing what the manager considered to be the injustice of the penalty award which led to Willie van der Kaylen striking a killer blow past Paul Bradshaw 14 minutes from time (picture below) after the scores had been level at the three-quarter stage.

Wolves, who had equalised through a fine header by Aston Villa's former European campaigner Andy Gray, could do no better than halve the deficit in the return leg a fortnight later – a notable evening on which the Molineux floodlights briefly went out.

To Mel Eves, whose goal in the second leg raised hope, goes the honour of being Wolves' last scorer in major European competition, the club having played 32 games in all across seven campaigns. Derek Dougan, who netted home and away against Den Haag, is the club's top marksman in Continental competition with 12 goals – five more than Peter Broadbent.

DAVID DRYER · SPORTS TRAVEL LIMITED

UEFA Cup
1st round · 1st leg
17th Sept 1980

P.S.V. EINDHOVEN
V
WOLVERHAMPTON WANDERERS

Braddy beaten

An author-taken photo from 2013 of Den Haag's current stadium - the one Wolves lost at on their latest visit. Ironically, the red-shirted visitors in the picture are PSV Eindhoven.

A return trip in 2005 to the Dutch capital, The Hague, left unhappy memories for Wolves fans. Glenn Hoddle's side flew out as part of their pre-season build-up and lost 3-0 to the same host club amid some crowd trouble.

On an individual note, Ted Farmer scored a hat-trick in Rotterdam in 1961 for a victorious England under-23 side who were captained by Bobby Moore and coached by Billy Wright. Dick Le Flem, the winger who was destined to move to Molineux from Nottingham Forest two years later, was also in the line-up.

As for Graham Taylor's touchline rant at a linesman in the same stadium in 1993, the least said the better.....

FIND US KEEPERS!

There has been an element of double Dutch about Wolves' signing of goalkeepers over the last decade or two. Hans Segers, who heroically saved a Jimmy Floyd Hasselbaink penalty in the 1998 FA Cup quarter-final victory over Leeds at Elland Road, is from Eindhoven while Stefan Postma, who made more than 30 appearances for the club in the mid-noughties after arriving from Aston Villa, was born in Utrecht.

IRELAND

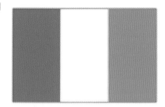

Never has Ireland been more popular with Wolves and their supporters than in the modern era. As a successful former Republic boss, it is perhaps no surprise that Mick McCarthy turned to the country named on his passport when it came both to searching for new signings and also in the important business of pre-season preparation.

McCarthy, seen above with Tommy Barratt and his granddaughter Taila Miller, is always welcome on that side of the water following his trips to World Cup finals as a player and a manager. He took Wolves there on pre-season trips three times in four years either side of the winning of promotion. And the club clearly put some sturdy roots down in the process. The habit has continued under Kenny Jackett – ironically a proud former Welsh international.

The Emerald Isle was a frequently chosen destination at the club long before Barnsley boy McCarthy was even born. Wolves went there in 1937, 1938 and as FA Cup holders in 1949. Major Frank Buckley, seen one in from the right, is the man in charge on the pre-war visit above.

Just over a decade later, Wolves proudly packed the Cup among their belongings and had it on

show when they beat a Munster Select XI 3-2 in Cork. But the man who had lifted it at Wembley three weeks earlier was not present, England calls taking Billy Wright off to Scandinavia instead. Bert Williams was also on the brink of an international place, so Dennis Parsons was in goal.

In their absence, Wolves also drew 1-1 with a Dublin Bohemians side containing eight regular Football League players, Leslie Smith scoring in both that game and the second one. Malcolm Clews, a Tipton-born inside-forward who was still in his teens, appeared in both matches and netted in the second, although he would leave the club after playing only one League game.

An off-duty perk for the Wolves party in Ireland in 1949....Joe Gardiner (left) and Bill Shorthouse (right) have Express & Star correspondent Phil Morgan (one in from the right) as company at the head of the field on a trip to a country where horse racing is a way of life.

Jack Howley, Wolves' loyal secretary for 20 years from a few months before the 1949 trip to Ireland — and on the Molineux staff for nearly half a century. Minding the keepsakes from foreign travels was always a passion.

Ireland became a welcome refuge in the savage winter of 1962-63 when Stan Cullis responded to the numerous domestic postponements by decamping there with his ring-rusty players for match practice.

Only once from mid-December to mid-February did the elements relent sufficiently for them to play a League game and their programme was in huge turmoil. So much so that, on one Thursday, they didn't know whether they would be playing at Nottingham Forest, at home to Ipswich or against Coventry in Ireland on the following Saturday.

Above: Somewhere on that busy programme front cover is a mention of who the match is actually between! Right: Terry Wharton takes on Coventry's Brian Hill in the mud. Below right: The teams, with changes.

With no thaw in sight, Cork Hibernians were delighted to extend a hearty 'cead mile failte' to both they and Jimmy Hill's Sky Blues, albeit also with an apology that their own Flower Lodge ground was in a state after a rise in temperature and heavy rain. Cullis bore some of the brunt by sitting on an uncovered bench in a downpour.

Wolves won 3-0 against their Third Division South opponents, with whom they had flown out of Elmdon on match day. They then beat them again in Belfast 11 days later, this time by 6-3.

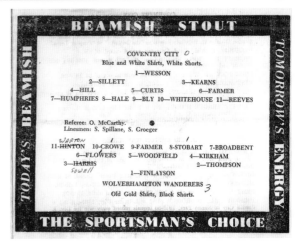

47

O'Brien's goal wins for Bohemians

BOHEMIANS 1
**WOLVERHAMPTON
WANDERERS** 0

BOHEMIANS survived severe Wolverhampton pressure in the second half at Dalymount Park last night and gained a memorable win over the newly-promoted English first division side. A splendid goal from Rocky O'Brien in the 28th minute inspired the home side throughout the remainder of the first half and they might have been more than a goal ahead had not goalkeeper Paul Bradshaw tipped a David O'Brien header over the bar in the 39th minute.

Showing remarkable commitment and no little skill Bohemians presented Wolverhampton with quite a few problems to sort out if they wish to make an impression in the English league in the coming season.

Showing signs of extreme panic at times the visitors lost the composure which they had in the first twenty minutes and allowed themselves to lose concentration as the spirited home side took the game to them.

But Bohemians also had their moments of luck and none more so than nine minutes after the interval when goalkeeper Dermot O'Neill had to dive sharply to avert danger from a Dave Connell headed back pass. And in the 72nd minute O'Neill had to go full length to scramble the ball around the post for a fruitless corner.

Bohemians almost made it 2-0 five minutes from time when a brilliant move involving Tony Hynes, Liam O'Brien and Paul Doolin saw Doolin heading the ball towards goal but Paul Bradshaw saved smartly.

BOHEMIANS — D. O'Neill, D. Connell, T. Hynes, B. Murphy, G. Lawless, P. Doolin, L. O'Brien, J. McCormack, J. Raynor, D. O'Brien, M. Shelly.

Subs—P. Walsh for Connell (70th minute), P. Hughes for Sherry (67th minute)

WOLVERHAMPTON WANDERERS — P. Bradshaw, J. Humphrey, P. Daniel, G. Smith, J. Pender, G. Palmer, K. Hibbitt, W. Clarke, M. Eves, D. Rudge, T. Towner.

Wolves returned to Ireland for a three-match tour under Graham Hawkins just before their brief return to the top flight in 1983. Between an easy win against Drogheda and a draw with Athlone came a 1-0 loss against Bohemians in Dublin, from which a match report is shown left. The photos on this page illustrate the sun-filled trip to the country in 2000, when Colin Lee's side kept a clean sheet in all three matches - a 2-0 victory over Waterford (below), a 0-0 draw in Cork (bottom) and a 2-0 Friday night win against Kilkenny (top picture on the opposite page). A feature of the trip was that Ade Akinbiyi flew home early to join Premier League newcomers Leicester.

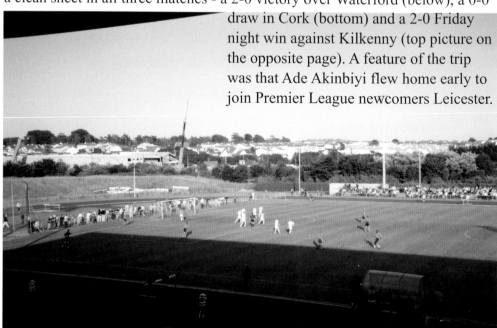

Fast forward a few years and Wolves were seen plenty over the Irish Sea. Secretary Richard Skirrow has reason to remember the 2007 visit based in Portmarnock – he made an overnight excursion with the forms for Stephen Elliott's transfer from Sunderland. There have also been three trips centred on Kildare, one a training camp only, with the presence at Molineux of former Irish boss Mick McCarthy (seen below 'directing the traffic' on one of those stays) an obvious pull in the club being so welcome. Kenny Jackett followed suit in 2014 with a trip to Malahide, from where they branched out to record goal-laden wins over Shamrock and Bohemians.

SOUTH AFRICA

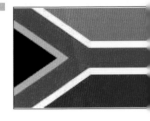

Have Wolves left a better impression anywhere on the planet on tour than they did in South Africa well over half a century ago?

Two trips to the republic, six years apart, brought them 18 wins out of 18 and a host of admirers. It was even the location that Billy Wright credited with the rediscovery of his imperious form following a personal crisis of confidence early in 1951.

Peter Broadbent turned 18 on the club's first visit to the continent of Africa and, when fellow forward Jimmy Mullen flew home early from the 12-game stay because of the birth of his second child, he said: "It must be the most wonderful trip any side from here has ever had in a foreign country."

Wolverhampton Wanderers
South Africa 1951

Ready to rock the republic.....back row (from left): Jesse Pye, Norman Deeley, Roy Pritchard, Joe Gardiner (trainer), Dennis Parsons, Johnny Walker, Jack Short. Middle row: Leslie Smith, Bill Shorthouse, Bill Baxter, Roy Swinbourne, Angus McLean, Sammy Smyth, Eddie Russell, Jimmy Mullen. Front row: Stan Cullis (manager), Peter Broadbent, Charles Hunter (director), Billy Wright, James Marshall (director), Jimmy Dunn, Eddie Fisher (South Africa team manager). Below right: One of the gifts presented to the tourists during their victorious trip.

In an end-of-season stay that lasted a month and a half, Wolves darted from Johannesburg to Durban, Pretoria, Cape Town, Port Elizabeth and back to Joburg, with other stop-offs in between. And, everywhere they touched down, it rained goals.

Even Stan Cullis got in on the act against South West Districts in Mossel Bay. He not only lined up in Wolves' 11-0 victory by way of a belated curtain call to his playing career but also used it to score his only senior goal for the club. His side managed exactly 50 goals on their 1951 trip, which was the club's first trip beyond Europe's boundaries.

Roy Swinbourne is down but was soon back on his feet and ended the tour with 17 goals. Right: A warm welcome awaits Wolves, especially skipper Billy Wright, from ex-pat workers in Durban, where Wolves played two games almost a month apart.

South African tour of 1951

May 19 (Johannesburg): *Southern Transvaal 1 Wolves 4* (Pye, Swinbourne 2, Smyth)

May 24 (Bloemfontein): *Orange Free State and Basutoland 0 Wolves 4* (Swinbourne 2, Smyth, Walker)

May 26 (Durban): *Natal 1 Wolves 3* (Swinbourne 3)

May 31 (Pretoria): *Northern Transvaal 0 Wolves 7* (Smith, Swinbourne 2, Pye 3, Broadbent)

June 2 (Cape Town): *Western Province 0 Wolves 4* (Walker, Pye 2, Smith)

June 6 (Mossel Bay): *South West Districts 0 Wolves 11* (Walker 3, Broadbent 3, Mullen, Dunn 2, Smyth, Cullis)

June 9 (Port Elizabeth): *Eastern Province 1 Wolves 5* (Mullen, Pye, Swinbourne, Dunn, Smith)

June 13 (East London): *Border Frontier State 0 Wolves 2* (Baxter, Walker)

June 16 (Benoni): *Eastern Transvaal 0 Wolves 13* (Swinbourne 6, Pye 4, Smith 2, Wright)

June 20 (Pietermaritzburg): *Natal 1 Wolves 2* (Smyth 2)

June 23 (Durban): *South Africa 1 Wolves 4* (Smith 2, Swinbourne, Pye)

June 30 (Johannesburg): *South Africa 0 Wolves 1* (Dunn)

'It must be the most wonderful trip any side from here has ever had in a foreign country' - Jimmy Mullen

SETTLING FOR A LIFE OF WARMTH

It hasn't been a one-way street as regards the movement of players between Wolverhampton and South Africa. Although Eddie Stuart, Des Horne and Cliff Durandt represent the club's highly successful plundering of emerging talent from that part of the world, others have gone in the opposite direction. Among the former Wolves players who have settled permanently in South Africa are Johnny Kirkham, Mike Kenning and reserve Mike Collins while a host of others, like Terry Wharton, Les Cocker, Barry Stobart, Micky Lill, Fred Kemp, Peter Withe and Derek Dougan served clubs over there.

n interesting variation
n the spelling of a
ero's name....

Wolves welcomed the South African XI for a game to officially switch on Molineux's floodlights and won the first of their League Championship titles before they returned to the republic for a second tour of duty in 1957 – one that also took in Rhodesia.

There were only the eight games this time and the players were away for just under a month – was Stan Cullis going soft on them? Once more, though, the goals rained in.

No-one enjoyed the stay more than Johannesburg-born Eddie Stuart, who was captain for much of the trip because Billy Wright was travelling elsewhere on the globe with England. Amid echoes of Mullen's 1951 comment, Stuart said: "It was the best tour we ever had."

The "WOLVES"
in
Southern Africa
1957

No. 9

S.A. TOUR

With the compliments of your Coca-Cola Bottler

Mon. 13th		
8.45 a.m.	Proceed by motor coach to Louis Botha Airport.	
10.00 a.m.	Depart DURBAN by S.A. Airways Flight S.A.319.	
3.30 p.m.	Arrive CAPE TOWN (D. F. Malan Airport). Proceed by motor coach to and stay at the International Hotel.	
Wed. 15th	*MATCH AGAINST WESTERN PROVINCE.*	
Thurs. 16th		
3.45 p.m.	Proceed by motor coach to D. F. Malan Airport.	
5.00 p.m.	Depart CAPE TOWN by S.A. Airways Flight S.A.302.	
8.45 p.m.	Arrive JOHANNESBURG (Jan Smuts Airport). Proceed by motor coach to and stay at the Victoria Hotel.	
Sat. 18th	*MATCH AGAINST A SOUTH AFRICAN XI.*	
Wed. 22nd		
10.15 a.m.	Proceed by motor coach to Jan Smuts Airport.	
11.45 a.m.	Depart JOHANNESBURG by S.A. Airways Flight S.A.250.	
1.50 p.m.	Arrive BULAWAYO (Kumalo Airport). Proceed by Central African Airways transport to and stay at the Cecil Hotel.	
Fri. 24th	*MATCH AGAINST SOUTHERN RHODESIA.*	
Sat. 25th		
5.45 a.m.	Proceed by Central African Airways transport to Kumalo Airport.	
6.30 a.m.	Depart BULAWAYO by Central African Airways Flight C.E.640.	
8.00 a.m.	Arrive SALISBURY.	
9.15 a.m.	Depart SALISBURY by Central African Airways Flight C.E.900.	
10.50 a.m.	Arrive NDOLA. Proceed by private transport to KITWE and stay at the Nkana Hotel.	
Sun. 26th	*MATCH AGAINST NORTHERN RHODESIA.*	
Wed. 29th		
a.m.	Proceed by private transport to Ndola Airport.	
10.35 a.m.	Depart NDOLA by Central African Airways Flight C.E.804.	
3.20 p.m.	Arrive NAIROBI.	
8.15 p.m.	Depart NAIROBI by S.A. Airways Flight S.A.214.	
Thurs. 30th		
11.10 a.m.	Arrive LONDON.	

APRIL, 1957

Sat. 27th		
1.00 p.m.	Depart LONDON by air.	
Sun. 28th		
1.35 p.m.	Arrive JOHANNESBURG (Jan Smuts Airport). Proceed by motor coach to and stay at the Victoria Hotel.	

MAY, 1957

Sat. 4th	*MATCH AGAINST SOUTHERN TRANSVAAL.*	
Wed. 8th	Proceed by motor coach to PRETORIA.	
	MATCH AGAINST COMBINED NORTHERN AND EASTERN TRANSVAAL.	
	Return to hotel after the match.	
Thurs. 9th		
6.00 a.m.	Proceed by motor coach to Jan Smuts Airport.	
7.45 a.m.	Depart JOHANNESBURG by S.A. Airways Flight S.A.317.	
9.30 a.m.	Arrive DURBAN (Louis Botha Airport). Proceed by motor coach to and stay at the Park View Hotel.	
Sat. 11th	*MATCH AGAINST NATAL.*	

On parade on tour. Back row from left: Stan Cullis (manager), Jimmy Mullen, Gwyn Jones, Peter Broadbent, Malcolm Finlayson, Jimmy Murray, Noel Dwyer, Gerry Harris, Ron Flowers, Joe Gardiner (trainer). Front: George Showell, Harry Hooper, Colin Booth, Eddie Stuart, Bobby Mason, Norman Deeley, Eddie Clamp, Colin Tether.

Wolves, having finished only sixth in the First Division the previous season by way of a build-up to the resumed greatness that was to follow, quickly cut loose in the Southern Hemisphere.

They made light of playing in the altitude of Johannesburg by putting five past Southern Transvaal and, although the going was harder in nearby Pretoria, they triumphed again – this time with a lone strike by Jimmy Murray, the plunderer of 17 goals in 1956-57.

And when the tourists moved down to the coast, they really clicked into gear by beating Natal 5-1 in Durban and Western Province 6-0 in Cape Town.

...uvenirs from touring round South Africa......an attractive stand (above) that remains on ...play in one of Molineux's showcases, a programme from the game against the state of ...tal and a passport stamp from the republic. But, more than half a century on, this ...arent commercial endorsement (below), which has nothing to do with the 'Pink' back ...ne, looks less welcome – even from an era in which smoking was more acceptable.

1957
WOLVES
SOCCER
TEAM

Back Row L. to R.
J. Mullin
G. Jones
P. Broadbent
M. Finlayson
J. Murray
N. Dwyer
J. Harris
R. Flowers

Front Row L. to R.
G. Showell
H. Hooper
C. Booth
E. Stuart
(Captain)
R. Mason
N. Deeley
E. Clamp
C. Tether

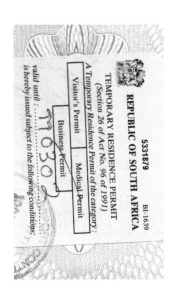

REPUBLIC OF SOUTH AFRICA
5331879   BI-1639

TEMPORARY RESIDENCE PERMIT
(Section 26 of Act No. 96 of 1991)
A Temporary Residence Permit of the category:

Visitor's Permit   Medical Permit

Business Permit

is hereby issued subject to the following conditions:

valid until:

22   SUNDAY TIMES, JOHANNESBURG, TRANSVAAL, MAY 5, 1957.

HAIL THE GREATEST FOOTBALL MACHINE TO VISIT SOUTH AFRICA IN POST-WAR YE

Murray's 5 for Wolves—Team of Dyn

S. TRANSVAAL . . 2, WOLVES . . 5

CALL them a team of mechanical footballers . . . call them human thoroughbreds . . . or even eleven dynamos . . . but whatever you may call them this Wolverhampton Wanderers side are the slickest, smartest and most penetrating soccer machine to visit South Africa since the war.

A Rand Stadium crowd of 25,000 saw them score five — all to centre-forward Jim Murray. — and give a wonderful exhibition of ball play at a tremendous speed on a greasy ground in the opening game of the seven-match tour against a game but obviously amateur bunch of footballers in the Southern Transvaal colours.

bove: A view from afar for Wolves' defenders on tour as
ay appears to be concentrated in the opposition half of the
eld, as usual.

eft: The South African press stated their view clearly enough
and this was only after the opening match!

elow left: Do this group look much different to footballers
day? There is an obvious love of the sun at the end of a hard
ason, some high jinks and the occasional show of vanity.
rom left are Ron Flowers, Colin Tether, Gwyn Jones, Eddie
lamp, Malcolm Finlayson, Eddie Stuart, Colin Booth, Joe
ardiner, Gerry Harris, Jimmy Murray and Bobby Mason.

bove right: Colin Booth pictured in kit and in isolation in
he of the stadiums Wolves graced — or is it Harry Hooper? A
sette from the tour is also shown.

ight: A nice keepsake from one of the three games the club
ayed in Johannesburg's Rand Stadium; another victory, of
urse.

A safe catch on the hard training grounds of South Africa by Malcolm Finlayson, who succeeded Bert Williams as Wolves' first-choice keeper in the second half of the 1950s and would win back-to-back League Championship medals in the two years following this long tour.

HIT OR MISS

Eddie Stuart – big man, big impact.

Des Horne – an FA Cup final winner.

Cliff Durandt – faced Wolves in his home country as a 16-year-old and subsequently brought back by boat but in the 'so-so' bracket.

Mark Williams – the mid-1990s forward flickered, then soon went out.

OH NO ... A SPURNED OPPORTUNITY
Peter Withe was signed from South African football on the recommendation of Derek Dougan but played only 17 games before going on to Birmingham and then to Nottingham Forest and Aston Villa, winning the League and the European Cup at the latter two clubs.

RHODESIA

At the end of the club's second long African tour, Billy Wright, God bless him, dutifully flew out for two farewell matches in Zimbabwe – a country we have been calling by its previous name for the purposes of this publication.

Although the World Cup finals in Sweden were a year or so away, Billy had been off playing for England but was able to line up against Southern Rhodesia in Bulawayo and Northern Rhodesia in Kitwe for matches that were both won by landslide double-figure goal hauls.

The skipper would like to have been playing in South Africa, too. It was there six years earlier that he had rediscovered his magnificent form after the tail end of the 1950-51 campaign had seen him locked in the worst personal slump of his outstanding playing career.

Norman Deeley, who had served in North Africa during the Suez Crisis, scored hat-tricks in each game in Rhodesia but fellow winger Jimmy Mullen went one better by netting four times in the second of them, having hit a brace in the first.

Familiar voices from another pink bit on the map!

Rhodesia may be a country more readily associated these days with cricket rather than football. But Wolves' players didn't feel alone when they touched down there almost 60 years ago for what remains the club's only trip to a now troubled country.

They were lifted by the sight of cheerful faces as they disembarked their plane in Bulawayo. Correspondents reported that a small group of immigrants from Wolverhampton offered them a warm welcome and were 'sporting gold and black favours.'

The club set something of a trend by visiting the country, the likes of Leicester, West Ham and, more unlikely still, Oldham then flying out to play prestige friendlies in the 1960s.

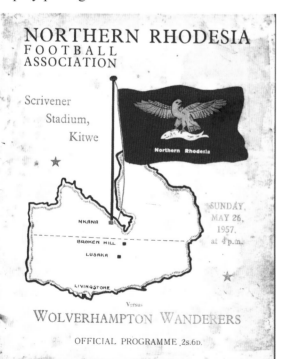

But Wolves' long journey home was nothing like the fun the tour itself had been.

It took all of 54 hours thanks to heavy flooding at Nairobi Airport, where the team touched down for refuelling, and a diversion via Uganda was necessary.

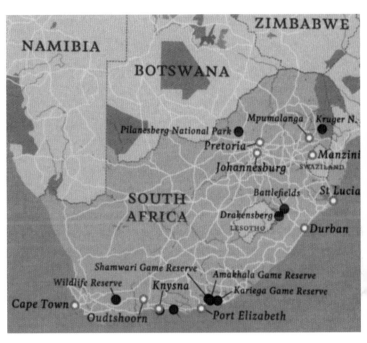

Again, the side's overall playing record in Africa was spectacular. They produced a 100 per cent winning record, this time with just the 49 goals rattled in!

But did Wolves come home jaded? Were they leg-weary for the following season? Not a bit of it. They won 6-1 and 5-0 in their opening two home fixtures of 1957-58 and lifted the title once more.

1957 tour results

May 4 (Johannesburg): *Southern Transvaal 2 Wolves 5* (Murray 5)

May 8 (Pretoria): *Combined Northern and Eastern Transvaal 0 Wolves 1* (Murray)

May 11 (Durban): *Natal 1 Wolves 5* (Broadbent 3, Deeley 2)

May 15 (Cape Town): *Western Province 0 Wolves 6* (Mullen 2, Booth 2, Broadbent, Hooper)

May 18 (Johannesburg): *South Africa X1 1 Wolves 4* (Broadbent 3, Deeley)

May 21 (Johannesburg): *President's X1 3 Wolves 7* (Deeley 2, Murray 2, Mason 2, Showell)

May 24 (Bulawayo): *Southern Rhodesia 1 Wolves 10* (Deeley 3, Mullen 2, Broadbent 2, Murray, Turnbull og, Mason)

May 26 (Kitwe): *Northern Rhodesia 1 Wolves 11* (Mullen 4, Deeley 3, Murray 2, Booth 2)

AUSTRIA

"You'll like Mark McGhee – he does a good pre-season tour," an East Midlands source told Molineux journalists after the manager's bitter and controversial switch from Leicester to Wolves in December, 1995.

Seven months later, those words were proved correct as the Scot prepared his players in the shadow of the Austrian Alps for his first full season in charge.

After all those trips to Sweden, this was something different for the fans who avidly follow Wolves abroad as well as at home. By anyone's standards, the scenery was absolutely stunning. And they got to sample the manager's hospitality – he bought them all a drink on the final night after the road-show had moved into Germany.

As a test for the squad, the games were still comfortable enough – the first being played only a short walk from the team's hotel in the ski resort of Abtenau. But there was some despair when Tony Daley and Adrian Williams suffered serious injuries in quick succession in the same training session and had to be flown home early.

Dean Richards had an unhappy time, too, because of injury before toothache became another problem for him in the build-up to the Sunday night win in Spittal. But Wolves retained their 100 per cent record when they moved over the border for the other two games of their stay.

Right: The proof that the squad's tour base in 1996 was indeed a picture postcard setting.

Above: New signing Iwan Roberts leads a training drill taken by coach Mick Hickman on the training ground that was also used as the pitch for Wolves' easy win against Abtenau.

Opposite: The sort of Alpine backdrop that prompted Steve Claridge to say after touching down on arrival for Wolves' visit to Austria in 1998: "If you can't enjoy training here, you won't enjoy it anywhere."

McGhee, a good German speaker following his time as a player with Hamburg, seemed at home on the trip.

He used the local tongue to make one thank-you speech to his squad's hosts and took his players back to Austria and Germany two years later when coming up with an almost identical itinerary.

HIT OR MISS

Stefan Maierhofer – if only his impact had matched the size of his frame.

Opposite: Mark McGhee was looking downwards, as well as upwards, as he prepared in the summer of 1996 for his first full season as manager at Molineux. Left: The year is different – this is 1998 – but the scenery is the same. Above: Physio Barry Holmes irons out a last-minute problem with the hotel management as the team check out of their Alpine headquarters and prepare to set off for a game with Lask Linz and then onwards into Germany.

There was an interesting additional name on the 1998 tour list......that of Keith Andrews. The Irishman was still well short of his 18th birthday and was recovering from a long-term injury but he impressed the club's management enough for them to invite him aboard for a change of scenery as he continued his rehabilitation.

Curle persuaded to join tour party

Wolves skipper Keith Curle today set off on tour under a cloud – after 11th hour negotiations had succeeded in averting a dramatic pull-out.

Curle was unsure as late as last night whether he would take his place in Mark McGhee's 18-man squad for the four-match trip to Austria and Germany.

But, despite his angry outburst against the club and his weekend demand for a free transfer, he was in the party who checked in for a mid-morning flight from Birmingham to Salzburg via Amsterdam.

"I am under contract to Wolves and, under the terms of it, I am expected to go on tour," Curle said.

But it is clear the former England defender – one of the stars of Wolves' ultimately depressing 1997-98 season – was hoping he may have been on the move to another club instead of reporting for 12 days of intensive preparation with

By David Instone

Curle and managing director John Richards, who is also on the trip, have been involved in a bitter public slanging match over the last few days and it remains to be seen whether this is a fresh start or a temporary truce.

McGhee, who installed Curle as captain on last summer's tour of Scotland, was not involved in the stormy contract discussions on Friday and Saturday, during which Richards flatly rejected a request for a free transfer despite being unable to accommodate the player in his pursuit of a con-

A pre-departure contract row between skipper Keith Curle and managing director John Richards provided an interesting backcloth initially to the 1998 return visit to Austria, especially as the club's one-time record marksman turned up for the middle section of the tour.

McGhee insisted beforehand that tougher matches had been chosen in 1998 in order to get his squad 'up to speed' more quickly. His judgement was underlined by successive defeats in Austria against Wustenrot Salzburg and Lask Linz, with scenes from the Salzburg fixture appearing on this page and the top half of the one facing. The headline translates to: *Salzburg Pull Out Wolves' Teeth*.

Salzburger zogen Wölfen die Zähne

Lehener gewannen Test gegen Wolverhampton 2:0 — Geglückter Auftritt von Reid

Von Alexander Bischof

SALZBURG. Salzburgs Trainer Hans Krankl hatte vor dem Testspiel gegen die Wolverhampton Wanderers (1. englische Division/zweite Leistungsstufe) Brian Reid noch ordentlich „heißgemacht": „Die Partie ist für dich eine Frage der Ehre." Der Schotte, der am Mittwoch gegen die „Wölfe" getestet wurde, nickte wissend, als wollte er sagen: „Keine

wann fast jedes Kopfballduell. Reid könnte jedenfalls der von Krankl gesuchte Manndecker sein.

Bei der Stürmersuche hoffen die Lehener nach wie vor darauf, daß Teamspieler Herfried Sabitzer das Angebot annehmen wird. Sabitzer, mit dem Mittwoch erneut verhandelt wurde, sah die Partie von der Tribüne aus. „Solange er noch bei keinem anderen Verein unterschrieben hat, ist er ein Thema für uns", meinte

fenberger, Aufhauser, Nikolic und Ibertsberger sorgten hingegen dafür, daß die Krankl-Elf von der ersten Minute an tonangebend war. Auch körperlich hinterließen Hütter & Co. einen starken Eindruck.

Edi Glieder, der wieder überaus agil wirkte, krönte seine gute Leistung mit dem Führungstor, nachdem Ibertsberger die Vorarbeit geleistet hatte (19.). Ein Zusammenspiel der beiden eingewechselten Kitzbichler

The Lehener Stadium, where the Salzburg game was played, was demolished in 2006 and became a futuristic shopping and library complex. Part of the pitch and terracing remained, though, as a reminder of the venue's past use.

There was the usual Austrian injury woe as Steve Sedgley and Dougie Freedman this time became the men who needed early flights back.

The game against Lask (below) came on the Saturday afternoon Wolves checked out of their idyllic base in Lofer and was moved 30 miles from Linz to the town of Grieskirchen near the German border.

When the games really mattered in Austria in decades past, Wolves weren't based in the mountains at all – but the capital city of Vienna.

The club's first trip was back in August, 1954, when they faced First Vienna in a game to celebrate their hosts' 60th anniversary. The English champions were held to a 2-2 draw in a downpour at the unprotected Prater Stadium – venue for both the 1964 European Cup final and the 1970 European Cup Winners' Cup final between Manchester City and Gornik Zabrze.

But Austrian football was on a high at the time and the praise from the home keeper suggested it was a good result. Speaking of Stan Cullis's men, he said: "They are the best English team seen in Vienna since the war."

Wolves' only competitive visit to the country came with their debut in the European Cup Winners' Cup in 1960 and meant a first flight for emerging centre-forward Ted Farmer.

Only ten teams played in that founder season of the competition, so FA Cup holders Wolves went in at the quarter-final stage. They certainly did things the hard way against FK Austria, losing the away first leg 2-0 after hitting the woodwork four times, only to rattle in five goals in the return more than a month and a half later.

Press coverage of the European Cup Winners Cup tie in Vienna .....from the Express & Star (above) and one of the Austrian papers (left). It calls goal-getter Ted Farmer a second Nat Lofthouse – the original Lion of Vienna.

DENMARK

KØBENHAVN

Wolves' party prepare for departure (below) to Scandinavia in 1954. Competing with Stan Cullis in the trilby stakes at the foot of the plane steps is the Express & Star correspondent Phil Morgan.

Three times in the 1950s, Wolverhampton Wanderers were able to plan summer travels with the tag 'English League champions' happily prefixing their name.

On the first of those occasions, 1954, they included two games in Denmark in a three-match end-of-season Scandinavian tour for which they were considerably depleted.

Johnny Hancocks was a reluctant and very occasional flier and Billy Wright, Jimmy Mullen and Dennis Wilshaw were away with England preparing for that summer's World

Wolves were able to pay their solemn respects to the hosts during their 1954 tour. The day before their final fixture was May 5, Danish Liberation Day, so director Charlie Hunter laid a wreath on behalf of the club at the Danish War Memorial in Copenhagen.

Cup finals in Switzerland. In addition, Bert Williams stayed at home, as well as Bill Slater, for business reasons, and Nigel Sims was on Young England duty, so Irishman Noel Dwyer kept goal and Bill Shorthouse expertly filled the role as captain.

Other lesser-known names in the tourists' squad were John Timmins, Bill Guttridge, Ron Stockin and Tommy McDonald.

Wolves were to decline an invitation to a tournament in Brazil later in the close season but found Denmark to their liking as they demolished Aarhus thanks to a hat-trick by Roy Swinbourne and a brace from Leslie Smith. Swinbourne received a silver spoon from a supporter as his side were praised by the media as being a more impressive side than previous visitors Moscow Dynamo and Juventus.

WOLVES KICK-OFF WITH 5–0 TOUR WIN

A SWINBOURNE hat-trick which won him a silver spoon was a feature of Wolves' impressive 5—0 win over a combined eleven in the first match of their Danish tour at Aarhus Stadium last night. The spoon was the gift of a supporter of two local clubs, ADF and AAA, for the best of the English players. It went deservedly to the Wolves leader, who, apart from scoring three goals, led the attack with skill and energy.

A 10,000 crowd turned out on a fine but cold evening.

There was some splendid goalkeeping by From, who made brilliant leaps to catch a Swinbourne header and late in the game dived at the feet of left-winger Smith, who scored the other two goals, to prevent the game's second hat-trick.

Within nine minutes of the start Swinbourne put Wolves ahead with a shot which eluded the goalkeeper's grasp and after 31 minutes Smith licked out of the goalkeeper's reach a forward pass from Clamp.

Six minutes later Swinbourne got the third when he beat a surprised goalkeeper by shooting as he was tackled

game, but their close passing, in which they persisted, always broke down against a strong Wolves defence in which Shorthouse was outstanding.

Wolves played some brilliant individual football, especially Swinbourne, Broadbent and Deeley. There was also a strong wing-half display from Flowers, who greatly impressed the crowd. Goalkeeper Dwyer showed up well in the few occasions he was needed.

PRESS TRIBUTE

After the match, Wolves director Mr. Charles Hunter received from the Aarhus clubs a piece of D...

Left and below: Press coverage of the champions' 1954 trip to Denmark, with the photograph showing Wolves centre-forward Roy Swinbourne as the filling in a Danish sandwich.

Danes greatly impressed by the Wolves

WOLVES are already looking forward to their next visit to Denmark. And that (writes "Commentator"), is surely the nicest way of saying how much they enjoyed the trip they have just completed.

The Danes liked them and they liked the Danes; they played good football which impressed the natives, and made many new friends. In other words, the whole thing was a tremendous success. From the point of view of football—and that was the primary reason we were there—one of the undoubted successes of the tour was Bill Shorthouse, who acted as captain in the absence of Billy Wright.

Unchanged side

He did the job splendidly, both on the field, where he was his customary determined self, and off, where he was the acme of courtesy, and a diplomatic link between players and officials, both English and Danish.

Mr. Cullis, wisely I thought, chose what he considered the best team and left them unchanged in the three games. They justified his confidence with 5–0 victories at Aarhus and Helsingborg and a 2—2 draw with the powerful Copenhagen representative side. Individual playing successes, I thought, were Flowers, Deeley and Smith.

Speed a big asset

Over-riding impression on the Danes was Wolves speed and their ability to keep it up for the whole 90 minutes. It was this facility which enabled them to...

Following a quick transfer by boat to Sweden for another five-goal flourish, Wolves headed to the Danish capital for their final game and had to settle for an entertaining draw against a Copenhagen XI.

Swinbourne, Smith, McDonald and the much-loved Peter Broadbent each scored in two of the games but no player netted in all three.

Bert Williams and Billy Wright lined up alongside each other in Denmark in 1952-53 in a fixture with a difference. They, as well as Alf Ramsey and Albion's Ray Barlow, played for the Football League against their counterparts from the Danish Combination in a game marking the 50th anniversary of the International Football Combination in early May.

Billy also played in England's 0-0 draw in Copenhagen in 1948, in a 5-1 win in 1955 in which Bill McGarry played as well and in a 4-1 victory in 1957 in which Duncan Edwards was among his team-mates. Much more recently, Steve Bull went on as a substitute there in 1989.

Above: The author's photo of the national stadium in Copenhagen – taken on Wolves' pre-season Scandinavian tour in 1994. Below: What's this? England internationals having to risk sea-sickness by travelling to a game in Denmark by boat during Wolves' glory years?

It was on a trip home from Denmark that Billy Wright learned he had been made England captain. As he boarded a bus in Wolverhampton and clutched the ham he had brought back for his landlady, Mrs Colley, he was greeted by conductress Helen Mearden and a copy of that night's Express & Star. There, in the stop press, was the announcement that he would lead the side out against Northern Ireland two weeks later.

It was almost a quarter of a century later before Wolves were back in Denmark – and then it was for only a fleeting stay.

Sammy Chung, who had coached in Scandinavia before linking up with Bill McGarry, had been in sole control for two years by the time of a five-match pre-season tour of Sweden in 1978 that had a friendly in the suburbs of the Danish capital tagged on the end of it. He is pictured looking relaxed (right) before the latter game, against Hvidovre.

Seen above on their way to a training session are Wayne Clarke and John McAlle, with the unmistakable figure of George Berry among those in the background. The match programme, complete with the bonus of a Manchester United v Wolves photo on the front, is seen right.

Welcome
to
Copenhagen

HOTEL
EUROPA
EF
EXCELSIOR

COLBJØRNSENSGADE 4-8
DK-1652 KØBENHAVN V
TEL +45 33 25 22 33
TEL +45 31 24 50 85
FAX +45 33 25 69 99
FAX +45 31 24 50 87
TELEX 15109

KVICKLY
præsenterer
ENGLÆNDER-FODBOLD

WOLVERHAMPTON
contra
HVIDOVRE

Torsdag den 27. juli 1978 kl. 19.00 - På Hvidovre Stadion.

No trip to Scandinavia is complete without one or two programme 'bloopers' and Wolves' 1978 hosts did not disappoint as, in the team line-ups, they gave us Mall Ewes, John Blake (rather than Black) and Jeff Palmer, who is seen walking off at half-time (right), with substitute Norman Bell and physio Kevin Walters in the foreground.

The fact Hvidovre away in 1978 was only a friendly was no reason for Mel Eves not to give everything. The sweat-soaked proud Wolves fan netted a treble in a 5-1 win in which Kenny Hibbitt (seen behind) was captain in his first full game after a broken ankle suffered the previous March. One of Eves' goals is shown at the top of the facing page.

Hvidovre, a club Old Trafford legend Peter Schmeichel served, was hardly a happy hunting ground for a Sweden-bound Wolves side in July, 1994 (below), although a Steve Bull brace saw them home 2-1. Graham Taylor's men had Jamie Smith and Lee Mills sent off.

Kenneth Munk longed to see his beloved Wolves playing in his home country. By the time they arranged their 1994 tour, though, he had fixed up a trip to the World Cup finals in America!

INDREJST
Kastrup
.1 9 JULI 1994
KØBENHAVNS POLITI
DANMARK   (35)

LUXEMBOURG

Lucky late goal, but the Wolves deserved to win'

THE big scoreboard at the Municipal stadium at Luxembourg Saturday reflected the significance of the meeting of Wolves the Racing Club of Paris.

On it, the teams were shown as Angleterre and France, and when the finish of an exciting game, it read 4—3 in favour of the English emphasised the last of the three effective blows struck by Wolves for country's soccer prestige and rounded off a fine season.

This was after the slick French side had gained a two-goal lead afte

Once or twice during the research for this project, we have stumbled upon a Wolves overseas game that previously appeared to have escaped the record books. One such fixture is the one referred to in the Express & Star cutting here – a meeting with Racing Club Of Paris in Luxembourg on May 7, 1955.

The visit to the duchy seems to have been a brief one, as is illustrated by the fact that the paper's correspondent, Commentator, was actually in Brussels when telephoning his match report back to Wolverhampton the next morning.

To fill in some gaps, we are happy to be a bit more functional with our coverage of this trip and dutifully record that Wolves were two down in 11 minutes to a club they had also faced in France before the war. Jimmy Mullen pulled one back with a header mid-way through the first half and Bill Slater equalised from a penalty just after the half-hour following a foul on the impressive Dennis Wilshaw.

Wilshaw expertly put Wolves ahead early in the second half, only for Racing to equalise after Bert Williams pushed a free-kick on to the bar.

The scoreline that is neatly recorded in lifelong fan Martin Wright's schoolboy scrapbooks (right) was rounded off as Tommy McDonald's corner was deflected in for the late winner.

SAT	MAY 7TH	1955.
	LUXEMBOURG.	
RACING CLUB of PARIS	v	WOLVES
3		4
Cisovski. (2).		Mullen.
Guillot.		Slater. (pen).
		Wilshaw.
		MacDonald.

USSR

Wolves have been there only once but the trip is as famous as any they have made anywhere on the globe. Sadly, the memories of a week and a bit behind Soviet lines aren't especially happy ones, on the pitch at least. The two games on the ground-breaking visit were in Moscow shortly before the 1955-56 season and left Stan Cullis and his men convinced they had to improve.

Priceless footage of the adventure survives, with a plummy voice saying 'Handle them carefully, pilot – those boys are insured for nearly a quarter of a million pounds' as their plane taxis towards the runway at London Airport. There are also numerous photos, either sight-seeing in this formidable capital city, on the way to it or at the stadium. Part of the reason for all the images is simple. The players each carried cameras presented to them after they beat Spartak at home 4-0 nine months earlier.

MOSCOW "TINGLING OVER WOLVES VISIT

Spartak hoping to revenge the defeat at Molineux

MOSCOW, THURSDAY.
A MOSCOW RADIO COMMENTATOR SAID LAST NIGHT THAT THE CITY WAS "TINGLING WITH EXCITEMENT" OVER THE FORTHCOMING VISIT OF THE WOLVES.
the United Kingdom half an hour was devoted

With friends before take-off are (back row from left): Jimmy Mullen, Stan Cullis, Eddie Stuart, Billy Wright, Ron Flowers. Front: Roy Swinbourne, Bill Shorthouse, Dennis Wilshaw, Peter Broadbent, Les Smith.

Above: Sightseeing time for Billy Wright, Bill Slater, Roy Swinbourne and Dennis Wilshaw. Note the cameras!
Below: A training break for Swinbourne and Wright in the heat of the Dynamo Stadium.

Wolves reported back for training ten days early to prepare, Norman Deeley and Tommy McDonald both missing some of the work as they were doing their National Service.

The players flew in two parties, staying overnight in Helsinki en route. A handful of fans, including Daisy St. Clair Mander, paid between £155 and £186 each to go. The Mayor of Wolverhampton, Alderman Frank Mansell, was among the travellers.

Wolves' squad, dressed in black blazers and grey flannels, touched down in Soviet aircraft, the first containing 11 of the 16 players. Maurice Smith in The People beat the patriotic drum by writing after a phone call to Cullis in Moscow the day before the first match: "You can put your last rouble on another prestige-punching Wolverhampton victory today."

The opening fixture, against Spartak, was played on a Sunday in front of 80,000. A red and white banner that hung under the 50ft high pictures of Lenin and Stalin read: 'Welcome to the Sportsmen of England.' Wolves' colours were lowered, though, by goals from Parshin (18), Netto (38) and Isaev (87), and the smiles on the faces of Bill Shorthouse, Roy Swinbourne and Dennis Wilshaw (left) soon vanished.

As Roy Peskett put it in the Daily Mail, the final 3-0 scoreline 'leered' from the giant scoreboard. 'What a flop – it might have been 6-0' was the headline on Desmond Hackett's piece in the Express. As for the heading below right, who knows?

Johnny Hancocks missed most of Wolves' trips to foreign fields in the 1940s and 1950s. The tiny winger was scared of flying and his reluctance to travel abroad – unless he could do so by sea and land – also took its toll on his promising career with England. He won only three full international caps, scoring twice against Switzerland on his debut – a game played at home (Highbury), of course, rather than in Zurich, Basle or Berne. Johnny listened to a radio commentary of the defeat to Spartak at the home of a friend while on a day trip to Rhyl.

ФИЗКУЛЬТУРА И СПОРТ

8 АВГУСТА 1955 г., № 220 (13518)

МЕЖДУНАРОДНАЯ ТОВАРИЩЕСКАЯ ВСТРЕЧА
ПО ФУТБОЛУ

«Вулвергемптон Уондерерс» (Англия) — «Спартак» (Москва)

They were a tight-knit group the 1950s Wolves, especially in Moscow!

'Not worth a rouble' was the damning headline on Bob Ferrier's piece after the Spartak mauling as Wolves retreated to the Intercontinental Hotel to lick their wounds. As the Soviets celebrated, there was also talk of a deciding third match between the two clubs within months after one thumping win apiece. "We can't leave things like this," Cullis said.

Wolves, who observed local custom by throwing bouquets of flowers to the crowd before the kick-off, were happily cast in the role of tourists between the fixtures and took in all the sights.

But, five days on from their Spartak slaughter, they had pride to salvage when they prepared to do battle with Moscow Dynamo.

Above: A programme from Wolves' visit east – even if it will be recognisable to most of us only by the date. Left: A small gift made to the visitors and still on show at Molineux 60 years later.

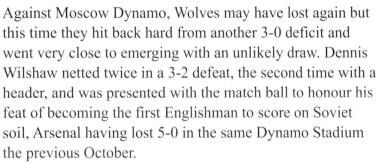

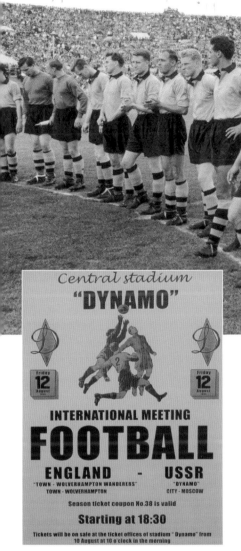

Against Moscow Dynamo, Wolves may have lost again but this time they hit back hard from another 3-0 deficit and went very close to emerging with an unlikely draw. Dennis Wilshaw netted twice in a 3-2 defeat, the second time with a header, and was presented with the match ball to honour his feat of becoming the first Englishman to score on Soviet soil, Arsenal having lost 5-0 in the same Dynamo Stadium the previous October.

Feodosov (14) and Kuznetsov (42 and 43) hit the goals that saw the hosts home but 'Salute these brave Wolves' and 'Moscow cheered gallant Wolves' were among the headlines reflecting a much, much better performance.

Wolves, hailed by the Daily Mail a few months earlier as 'Champions of the World' after beating Honved, had to travel a long way to meet their match during the glory years. But, for a few days in August of 1955, they were on the receiving end. In what Commentator in the Express & Star described as the club's greatest ever adventure, the scourge of Europe had themselves been humbled.

Top: Ready to contest national pride.....Stan Cullis and Joe Gardiner line up with their charges. Left: Bert Williams, Jimmy Mullen, Billy Wright, Les Smith and Ron Flowers relax in the stadium.

SPAIN

When it has come to trips to Spain, Wolves haven't messed about. They could have gone and played teams from the backwaters, concerning themselves mainly with getting a sun tan. But the reality has been totally different. They have taken the bull very much by the horns.

At opposite ends of 1957, they played friendlies in Valencia and Real Madrid, then the draw for the 1959-60 European Cup quarter-final sent them to the Nou Camp to face Barcelona.

And even a pre-season trip as League Cup holders in 1980 proved demanding enough for John Barnwell's squad to lose both games against formidable opposition.

Fans fly out to cheer up Wolves

From BILL HOLDEN   **Madrid, Tuesday**

THERE will be a miniature Molineux roar when Wolves run out at the Bernadeu Stadium for their game against European Cup holders Real Madrid here tomorrow.

Thirty-six Black Country fans were so anxious to watch Wolves that they chartered a special plane

hampton on October 17—and they defend their record of being unbeaten by foreign sides in Spain for five years.

Cullis will not finally decide his line-up until tomorrow.

But it IS certain that Billy Wright will be at centre half and playing for

ginal game against Real Madrid because he was with the England team.

One change is expected from the Wolves side which last Saturday shattered Preston's run of fifteen months without a home defeat.

Veteran Jimmy Mullen

Billy Wright, Peter Broadbent and Bobby Mason at leisure on Wolves' trip to Real Madrid in December, 1957 – a date the crack Spaniard side hoped to use to take revenge for their epic 3-2 defeat at Molineux a couple of months earlier. But Mason and Jimmy Mullen scored the goals in a draw as Stan Cullis's men heroically came out of the mouth-watering double-header with their noses in front. Billy had retired before the European Cup games against Barcelona but was a frequent flier to Spain on international duty.

A result to be proud of

It was inevitable that Stan Cullis would want his team to be challenged at their peak by sides from one of Europe's strongest football nations.

The initial test was failed as Wolves were beaten 3-1 by Valencia on their first visit to Spain but the result from their second game is worthy of displaying proudly here from a team-sheet souvenir of match night – and at every other possible opportunity.

As Real Madrid were at the time well under way in their historic feat of winning the European Cup in each of its first five seasons, Wolves' players considered themselves worthy of a celebratory drink after emerging from the Bernabeu Stadium with a 2-2 draw.

The trouble was they had ventured out into the early hours without the permission of Stan Cullis, who subsequently called them together to have his say on the escapade.

There was more than the odd raised eyebrow when the Iron Manager's biggest grumble with them was that he himself hadn't been invited out to let down what was left of his hair!

A grainy photograph of Billy Wright trying to repel a header by left-winger Gento on a night when the Bernabeu was lashed by monsoon-like conditions.

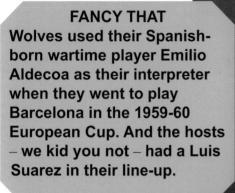

c. f. barcelona

N.º 148 10 febrero 1960 3 pta.

Alas, in competition rather than just with national pride at stake on a visit to Spain (main photo), the outcome was nothing like as satisfactory.

Barcelona, who were to visit Molineux in 1998 under Louis van Gaal for a pre-season friendly, thrashed the League champions 4-0 in the Nou Camp in front of nearly 100,000 and completed the kill amid another landslide in the West Midlands. Surviving highlights confirm the victors' football as being utterly spellbinding.

Barcelona

Without doubt, the last of Wolves' four European Cup ties (eight actual games) was a humbling experience. They were thrashed 9-2 on aggregate by Barcelona, the Spaniards then going on to be hammered by their arch rivals Real Madrid at the last-four stage.

Five men – Peter Broadbent, Gerry Harris, Norman Deeley, Ron Flowers and Bobby Mason – played in all Wolves' matches in the competition but were well into their retirement as players by the time the club were tempted back to Spain.

Stan Cullis addresses his players on the pitch on one of their 1950s visits to Spain. Colin Booth (left) looks a little distracted but Eddie Clamp, Bobby Mason and Malcolm Finlayson are much more attentive, judging by the evidence of this photo.

HIT OR MISS

Isidro Diaz – who?

Jesus Garcia Sanjuan – a goal on his debut proved a false dawn.

Fernando Gomez – a class act even late in his career.

Dani, una vez más, resolutivo

1-0: EL ATHLETIC SALVO EL HONOR ANTE EL WOLVERHAMPTON

Sólo 3.000 espectadores en un partido de discreta calidad

Bilbao, 8. (De nuestro colaborador.) – En San Mamés estábamos prácticamente en familia para presenciar el partido de consolación. Indudablemente la mala actuación ante los checos del Athletic habían ahuyentado a los aficionados. Apenas unos tres mil espectadores, que se fueron incrementando levemente a medida que transcurría el encuentro, fueron los que vieron el triunfo de su equipo. Tarde nublada, fresca y el terreno en excelentes condiciones.

Alineaciones:
ATHLETIC DE BILBAO: Aguirreoa; Urquiaga, Núñez, Goicoechea; De Andrés, Guisasola; Dani, Villar, Carlos, Sarabia, Noriega (Purroy).

WOLVERHAMPTON: Bradshan; Palmer (Carr), Parking, Daniel; Hugues, MacAllen; Brazier, Villasanz, Richards, Clarke, Thomas (Eves).

Andy Gray figuró como suplente y no salió al terreno de juego.

ARBITRO:

el resultado. Creemos que lo ingleses no podrán achacar al árbitro el motivo de su derrota.
GOL:
1-0: Minuto 20 del segundo tiempo. Noriega va por el ala derecha, hace una gran jugada, se atrae al defensa Parking, le «dribla», centra y en el mismo punto de penalty conecta un cabezazo enorme Dani que le vale el segundo gol particular, puesto que ya marcó ante el Bohemians.

El partido ha tenido poca historia, pero creemos, dicho sea con la mayor objetividad posible, que ha sido el triunfo del mejor, porque el Athletic ha estado mucho más seguro que ante los checos en su defensa y ha tenido una grata sorpresa en la actuación del joven Noriega quien, con el nueve a la espalda en partidos anteriores, ha llevado el número once, se ha desplazado muy bien por las alas derribando su puesto con Dani y, en suma, el equipo inglés se ha visto desbordado, aun cuando no se haya visto gran juego.

Lo cierto es que el enorme esfuerzo por levantar un resultado

decididamente en la segunda hacia la meta del portero bradshan. Además Sarabia, que había tenido una primera parte negra, con cansancio, desangelado, en la segunda realizó dos jugadas de maestro que a punto estuvieron de aumentar el marcador. En el minuto 20 llegaba como decíamos, el gol de Dani y el Athletic ya conservaría esta ventaja.

No ha sido convincente la actuación de los bilbaínos en su trofeo, el éxito económico ha brillado por su ausencia, pero en todo caso a Senekowichts le queda todavía la esperanza de la actuación de los jóvenes, porque también Purroy, en el poco tiempo que salió, estuvo bien y Urquiaga, el olímpico, el internacional, sigue afianzándose en su puesto. También hay que destacar el gran trabajo de Dani, trabajo que nos provocó a los medios informativos una gran polémica a la hora de decidir, para el trofeo que otorgaba una marca comercial, quién era el mejor jugador, si él o el alemán Lienen. Al final nos decidimos, quizá para evitar suspicacias, por este último que ha cuajado una gran actuación.

After a gap of nearly 20 years, Wolves headed well away from the holidaying hordes as they descended on Bilbao in the shadow of the Pyrenees. There were no memorable results this time as they lost by the odd goal to both Borussia Monchengladbach and Athletic Bilbao on successive days of a 1980 pre-season tournament. The latter club had been managed by Ronnie Allen following his sacking by Wolves late in 1968. The Spanish press came up with the headline 'Athletic keep pride intact against Wolverhampton' and the sub-heading 'Only 3,000 spectators at low-key game'.

Wolves haven't played in the country since, although Dave Jones took his squad to Jerez in 2003 for a training camp prior to the club's first Premier League season and Glenn Hoddle did the same two years later, a training scene from the latter trip being pictured above.

WEST GERMANY

For a club who had been the scourge of Europe under Molineux's intoxicating floodlights, Wolves made a pig's ear of their first entrance into the official organised continental competition they had been championing for years.

The draw for the opening round of the 1958-59 European Cup paired the Football League champions with Schalke 04, based in the industrial heartland in the city of Gelsenkirchen.

And it was an unhappy baptism, with a 2-2 draw at Molineux – based on a Peter Broadbent brace – followed by an odd-goal defeat in a return only six days later in which the visitors' goal came from the little-known Allan Jackson. It wasn't even as though Wolves had lost to a particularly strong side. Schalke crashed out 4-1 against Atletico Madrid in the next round.

An author-taken photo of the Gelsenkirchen stadium during the European Championship clash between West Germany and Denmark in 1988. On his visit, he was armed with a plaque from Molineux and asked to present it to hosts Schalke on Wolves' behalf as a way of keeping alive connections between the two clubs.

Bert Williams didn't play for Wolves or England in Germany but had interesting experience there in a post-war clash. He lined up for an FA XI against a Combined Services XI in Dusseldorf in November, 1945 – or against a Rhine Army team as some reports called them. The hostilities having ended only six months earlier, though, it was an allied line-up and not a German one. Jesse Pye (then of Notts County but later of Wolves) was also in the FA side, as was Billy Wright, and they finished 5-2 victors, watched by a 40,000 crowd.

The Schalke tie wasn't Wolves' first venture into Germany in 1958. A fortnight after lifting the First Division title by five points, they had won 4-3 in a friendly against Stuttgart at the mid-point of a five-match European tour that also took them to Switzerland and Belgium. The awful memory of Munich the previous February saw to it that Wolves made travel plans

that would seem bizarre now. Their 23-strong party flew on separate planes throughout the tour until they made a two-leg trip altogether from Stuttgart to Brussels via Frankfurt.

Destination-wise, there was a feeling of déjà vu 12 months later as the club again walked off with English football's top prize, then retraced familiar steps on their travels. This time, they lost to Stuttgart but won well against First Nuremberg after a handsome victory in Switzerland.

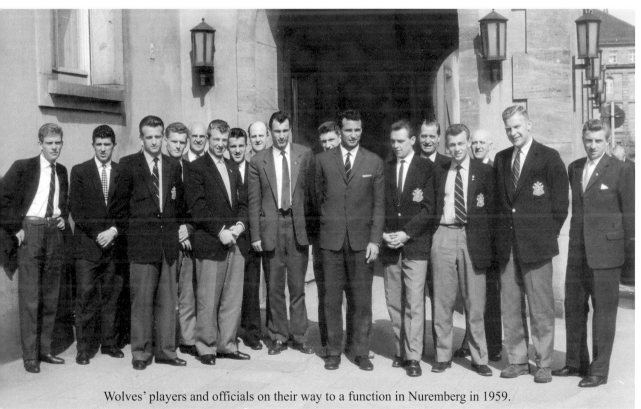

Wolves' players and officials on their way to a function in Nuremberg in 1959.

The Germans saw a very different Wolves on the club's mid-1960s visit. Stan Cullis had not long been dispensed with and the bitter taste of relegation was still in Molineux mouths as a squad preparing for Second Division combat contested a pre-season match against Kaiserslautern in August, 1965. A large group of players are pictured in their club gear on the left.

It was a happy trip, too, with goals by George Miller, Peter Knowles and Hugh McIlmoyle bringing them their first victory on the European mainland since the Nuremberg game six years earlier.

Cubs who grew up into Wolves

Kenny Hibbitt, Jeff Wealands, Jimmy McVeigh, Peter Eastoe, Jimmy Seal and Bertie Lutton were part of a Wolves squad who went to West Germany in May, 1969, for two youth tournaments under the management of Dave Maclaren and club secretary Phil Shaw. The squad were among the also-rans in both but Hibbitt was named player of the tournament first time round, a friendly in Karlsruhe also being arranged in between the competitions. McVeigh, seen above the left shoulder of keeper Wealands, was found to be a month too old and couldn't play in either tournament.

There was an unhappy follow-up to the 1965 trip to Kaiserslautern when Wolves were beaten 2-0 in Stuttgart in the summer of 1970. That was followed by a crushing defeat in Hanover and meant Wolves said a rueful Auf Wiedersehen to a country no first-team squad from Molineux would see again for more than 25 years.

But David Kelly, then with Walsall, went off to Euro 88 with the Republic of Ireland and is seen above having his photo taken in Stuttgart by Express & Star man Paul Turner.

Top-flight football had long disappeared off the Molineux landscape by the time Mark McGhee opted for Germany for the second half of four-game tours in both 1996 and 1998.

On each occasion, Wolves emerged with 100 per cent records, although it should be stressed that the calibre of opposition was nothing like that encountered by their predecessors.

McGhee saw his side master lower-division duo Kotzting and Weismain in his first summer in the job while Carl Zeiss Jena and Union Berlin were defeated two years later.

Where to place the Jena game in this book was a complicated issue. Although it was played after unification, we felt we had to include it in the same section as the 1971 clash with the same opponents, especially as it took place in the old East Germany.

HIT OR MISS

Jens Dowe (pronounced duvet) – nicht so gut. Signed as cover by Mark McGhee in 1996, he soon had his unhappy Molineux career put to bed.

Robert Niestroj – anyone even remember him?

Above: Wolves on their way to a 3-1 victory over Kotzting in 1996. Below: Despair for Mike Stowell and the players in front of him as Mark McGhee's side trail against Union Berlin in 1998. But they rallied to win 2-1.

SWITZERLAND

England were the newly-crowned world champions when Wolves last visited Switzerland – and the national celebrations were possibly a moot point with two Scots in Ronnie Allen's party, keeper Dave Maclaren and centre-forward Hughie McIlmoyle! Presumably, Englishmen Dave Wagstaffe, Graham Hawkins, Joe Wilson and Mike Bailey (pictured above on a sightseeing walk) were happy enough with the outcome.

The Jules Rimet Trophy had been won less than a fortnight before the Alpine excursion, on which Wolves warmed up with mixed results for what proved to be a 1966-67 Second Division promotion-winning campaign. They lost comfortably to Zurich and then drew with Servette.

The trip was virtually a swansong on the playing side of the club for Maclaren, who is pictured left on tour from Molineux in the mid-1960s. He had so impressed Southampton even in Wolves' 9-3 humiliation at The Dell early in 1965-66 that he was subsequently signed by them.

Another wise old head playing a Swiss role was Ron Flowers, who stood alone as a survivor from the club's previous trip there in 1958. But experienced centre-half Dave Woodfield pulled out shortly before departure with a knee injury suffered in training.

Les Wilson, who had considered returning permanently to Canada over the summer because of homesickness, was drafted in, then Wolves had another setback shortly after arrival when winger Pat Buckley badly gashed his shin while posing for a photo by the pool at the squad's lakeside hotel.

Heavy rain meant Wolves officials had to send for a set of plastic umbrellas before the players could go on a boat trip organised for them and they were all at sea when beaten 3-1 by a Zurich side who had won the domestic league and cup double a few weeks earlier.

The hosts also had five members of the Swiss side who had played in that summer's World Cup finals and were managed by Laszlo Kubala, a member of the Barcelona squad who severely mauled Wolves in the 1959-60 European Cup.

Pictured enjoying the clean air are (back row, from left): Ron Flowers, Peter Knowles, Hugh McIlmoyle, Ken Knighton, Joe Wilson, John Holsgrove, Dave Wagstaffe, Dave Maclaren. Front: Bobby Thomson, Fred Davies, Graham Hawkins, Les Wilson, Terry Wharton, Ernie Hunt, Mike Bailey, Paddy Buckley.

Looking bright in white

Servette were formidable opponents, too, having finished runners-up in the two domestic competitions a few weeks earlier, but were pushed into a change of plan for Wolves' visit. The game between the clubs was scheduled for their home ground in Geneva but was switched to Lausanne, where the tourists were based.

MAN MOUNTAINS

Wolves didn't have top billing at their base in the Alps. West Ham, including their England heroes Bobby Moore, Geoff Hurst and Martin Peters, stayed in the same hotel before a pre-season game of their own. Despite having played major parts in the winning of the World Cup less than a fortnight before, the all-star trio played all three of their side's 1966 tour games, including one against Lausanne which was watched by several Wolves players.

Mike Bailey was a relative newcomer when he went off on tour with Wolves to Switzerland, having been signed less than six months earlier. The long-time skipper is pictured (above) at leisure on the city streets while (from left) Les Wilson, Fred Davies and John Holsgrove decided the hotel swimming pool (left) was a safe place to partially strip off and catch a little more sun. Holsgrove was delighted to be present after being left behind off the trip to West Germany the previous summer.

Preparing to enter a foreign field.....Ken Knighton (left), a Wolves tourist to North America and Canada in 1963, to West Germany in 1965 and to Switzerland in 1966, gets ready to make his entrance.

The Yorkshireman was a product of the famous Wath Wanderers nursery and, more than a decade later, would have been delighted to see some of his successors in the Molineux junior teams making a mark of their own.

Over Easter in 1976, the Wolves side pictured below and captained by Colin Brazier became the first English winners of a then 36-year-old youth tournament organised by Swiss club AC Bellinzonia. Wolves beat Rijeka of Yugoslavia 3-1 in the final, Brazier, Paul Moss and Steve Crompton scoring, having earlier defeated Varese and Ferencvaros, and drawn with Servette.

WORLD CUP WONDERS
Dennis Wilshaw and Jimmy Mullen had good reason to remember England duty in Switzerland. Both scored in a win over the hosts in Berne in the 1954 World Cup finals, with Billy Wright and Bill McGarry as colleagues.

Wolves had been a much more prominent force in the domestic game when they undertook their previous two first-team trips to Switzerland. They went there as League champions in 1958 to defeat both Grasshoppers in Zurich and then Servette in Geneva at the start of a mixed five-match European tour. It was while they were in Switzerland that they heard of the momentous FA Youth Cup final comeback against Chelsea at Molineux – news Stan Cullis described as the best he had ever received.

Wolves returned to the same country 12 months later for another end-of-season trip, this time crushing those Grasshoppers 6-2 in between two games in West Germany.

In 1958, Flowers found himself confronted by what became a familiar foe. Facing him in Switzerland as a guest player was none other than Sandor Kocsis, who had scored for Honved at Molineux in the famous 1954 friendly and would plunder four goals for Barcelona against Stan Cullis's side in their European Cup meeting at Molineux in 1959-60. At least Flowers helped keep the Hungarian goal-less in 1958.

Switzerland was twice Wolves' destination on youth trips in the early 1950s. An international one-day tournament took place in Zurich in mid-May, 1953, with a long series of shortened matches taking place and Wolves' first game starting at the unheard of time of 8.30am. The Wanderers cubs beat Wiedikon 1-0 through a Ron Howells goal and followed up by drawing 0-0 with Winterhur and Zurich Blue Stars. The side are shown in action there below.

Having finished second in their group and failed to progress, Wolves played Interlaken the following day, then travelled on to face a combined regional XI in Langenthal. The trip was rounded off by a May 18 game in Schaffhausen against a local club's juniors.

Wolves Juniors beat Bernese Boys 3-1 in Switzerland in May, 1951 – the day of a first-team draw at Sunderland. A bear on a stand sits in one of Molineux's showcases in commemoration of the game.

99

EAST GERMANY

Accusations and posturing in Wolves' UEFA Cup victory away to Carl Zeiss Jena in November, 1971, with Derek Dougan – not for the first time – acting as spokesman.

WALTER-ULBRICHT-STADION

Europa-Pokal der Landesmeister

Mittwoch, 30. September 1959, 16 Uhr

Wolverhampton Wanderers

gegen **ASK Vorwärts**

Programmheft DM 0,20

Wolves, having done much through their famous programme of floodlit friendlies to pioneer proper competition between clubs from different countries across the continent, headed behind the Iron Curtain for their second tie in an official European tournament.

After losing in West Germany the year before to Schalke, they were again left with work to do when beaten 2-1 at East German club Vorwaerts in the preliminary round of the 1959-60 European Cup. But the back-to-back League title winners, whose hard-man duo Eddie Clamp and Eddie Stuart are pictured above in all white change kit, got it right in the second leg at Molineux to go through on aggregate by the odd goal.

Wolves had no such discomfort on a return trip to the bleak landscape in 1971 – except for the inhospitable weather and a power shortage, that is.

When paired with Carl Zeiss Jena in the third round of the UEFA Cup in November and December, Bill McGarry's men found themselves having to contend with biting temperatures and a snow-covered pitch.

But they won 1-0 away (thanks to a John Richards goal) and 3-0 at home before the competition went into winter hibernation for two and a half months. Kenny Hibbitt is the man sliding in below on the difficult surface, with the partly visible Derek Dougan up in support.

Zimmernummer: *24*

GÄSTEAUSWEIS

Herr/Frau: *2 Gothard*

Zimmerpreis M

Anreisetag: **23 Nov 1971**

Abreisetag: **24. Nov 1971**

- Aushändigung des Zimmerschlüssels
- nur gegen Vorlage dieses Ausweises

**HO-HOTEL
INTERNATIONAL
WEIMAR**
AM HAUPTBAHNHOF
RUF 2162 / 2163

Richards went over some old ground more than 25 years later as Wolves' managing director when Mark McGhee's squad spent the second half of a pre-season tour in what used to be known as East Germany.

The 1998 Wanderers faced Carl Zeiss once more and Richards met two of the players he had faced in the early bloom of his playing career. But he was disappointed that the game, which was followed by one in Berlin two nights later, was played in the town of Schleiz, an hour south of Jena's base. At least the outcome was the same, Wolves won 1-0 and their centre-forward (guess who?) scored.

EINTRITTSKARTE

CARL ZEISS JENA FC — WOLVES

FC Carl Zeiss _ Wolverhampton
Jena   Wanderers FC

am Mittwoch, dem 22. Juli 1998,
auf dem Sportplatz
„Am Fasanengarten" in Schleiz
Anstoß: 19.00 Uhr

Vorspiel: FSV Schleiz I (16.30 Uhr)

Preis: 10,– DM   N⁰   123

A DEFENSIVE WALL NO MORE
Manchester-born Phil Painter, a regular on pre-season tours for many years, presented pieces of the demolished Berlin Wall to visitors from Molineux in 1998 and, in Sweden a year later, gave a glossy copy of the Berlin Wolves magazine to the club. From the latter tour, he had an 11-hour overnight train journey home.

Okay, we know East Germany was no more at the time of this featured clash with Carl Zeiss Jena in 1998 but it seemed odd mentioning the game in a separate section to the 1971 one against the same opponents.

JR carried out more than an ambassadorial role on tour in 1998. Having announced his late arrival with a vigorous run through the Austrian Alpine town of Lofer, where the players initially stayed for several days, he joined in one or two training sessions at the invitation of manager McGhee and, despite all that old trouble with his knees, didn't look anything like his then 49 years.

Wolves' other visit to East Germany came in the 1973-74 UEFA Cup, when, in the absence of the injured Richards, they lost 3-0 in the first leg at Locomotive Leipzig – their first loss in eight away matches in the competition. The deficit proved just too much to retrieve as they won the return 4-1 to go out on the away goals rule.

UEFA Pokalspiel
gegen

Wolverhampton Wanderers

Mittwoch,
den 24. Oktober 1973

1 FC LOKOMOTIVE LEIPZIG

17.00 Uhr
Zentralstadion

FUSSBALL-PROGRAMM

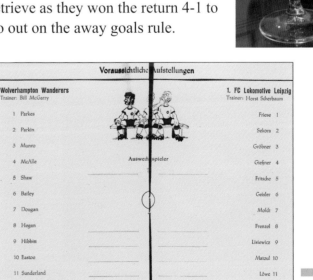

Voraussichtliche Aufstellungen		
Wolverhampton Wanderers Trainer: Bill McGarry		**1. FC Lokomotive Leipzig** Trainer: Horst Scherbaum
1 Parkes		Friese 1
2 Parkin		Sekora 2
3 Munro		Gröbner 3
4 McAlle	Auswechselspieler	Gießner 4
5 Shaw		Fritsche 5
6 Bailey		Geisler 6
7 Dougan		Moldt 7
8 Hegan		Frenzel 8
9 Hibbitt		Lisiewicz 9
10 Eastoe		Matoul 10
11 Sunderland		Löwe 11
Schiedsrichter: Minnoy (Belgien)		Linienrichter:

CANADA

For footballers who yearned to see the world, Wolverhampton Wanderers must have been the dream ticket.

Under Stan Cullis and Bill McGarry in particular, players collected stamps on their passports as quickly as they received winners' medals, the club's 1963 end-of-season tour taking them on another candidate for 'trip of a lifetime.'

A ten-game, month-long excursion was the first time Wolves had ever headed so far west and was split evenly between America and Canada, with five matches in each; all but one of them won.

Although Vancouver seemed to be a focal point on Wolves' long tour at the end of 1962-63 and is where the group photograph above is taken, the party's first point of disembarkation was Montreal, where there was the usual mix of training, match-day activity and socialising.

The newspaper-cutting pictures opposite show players and officials on a visit to the city, where

The party from Wolverhampton in front of Head Office building.

they were shown around by the top brass at Sun Life and treated to a roof-top view of the area.

Wolves won well in Montreal and put a spring in the heels of Ted Farmer, Peter Broadbent and Gerry Harris on the right. Farmer and Harris both scored in the 5-1 romp.

Wolves certainly clocked up the air miles in Canada and became well acquainted with an airline who had the colours of their next opponents Bangu well to the fore on their jets. Football staff shown on this embarkation photo are (left to right) Ted Farmer, Jimmy Murray, Fred Davies, Fred Goodwin, Barry Stobart and trainer Joe Gardiner.

WANDERERS WONDER IF THEY'LL REIGN

LEADING SHELTERED LIVES until they meet Bangu of Brazil Saturday are Wolverhampton Wanderers' goalie Fred Davies, manager Stan Cullis, and forward Chris Crowe. Wanderers arrived Tuesday, and went out to Empire Stadium to look over the field despite the rain. More than 20,000 are expected to watch Saturday's annual international exhibition match.

Following five matches in America, all won and the last of them in San Francisco, Wolves headed north to play their final four matches in Canada, where tough opposition lay in wait.

The Brazilians of Bangu were stocked with internationals and Wolves suspected as they checked into Vancouver's Devonshire Hotel after a two-hour stop in Seattle that they were in for a stern test in what the local press called the city's annual international exhibition match.

Both in Vancouver, though, and when they took the ferry across to Vancouver Island after this big Saturday night clash, they were made to feel at home among the high number of emigrants from Britain.

INTERNATIONAL SOCCER

WOLVERHAMPTON WANDERERS FOOTBALL CLUB—1962-63
BACK ROW: J. Kirkham, G. Harris, E. Farmer, F. Davies, J. Gardiner, trainer; M. Finlayson, R. Thomson, J. Harris, G. Showell.
CENTER ROW: F. Goodwin, W. Slater, R. Flowers, Mr. Stan Cullis, Manager; C. Crowe, T. Wharton, P. Broadbent.
FRONT ROW: P. McParland, J. Murray, C. Durandt.

WOLVERHAMPTON WANDERERS
(ENGLAND)
vs.
BANGU of BRAZIL

EMPIRE STADIUM, EXHIBITION PARK, VANCOUVER, B.C.

SATURDAY, JUNE 15, 1963, 8:30 P.M.

Price ... .33
Tax ... .02 **35c**

John Ireland (far right) and Stan Cullis are among those chatting with Vancouver officials (left) as they take an early look at the famous Empire Stadium four days before the clash with Bangu.

Pre-match formalities before Wolves v Bangu in Vancouver.....with chairman Jim Marshall preparing to do the honours (left) and number 15 Graham Hawkins about to try his hand as a photographer (below).

'Twas More Like a War Than a Mere Exhibition

The Canadian press didn't hold back in assessing a game in which Chris Crowe and Jimmy Murray twice put Wolves ahead. The headline above right says everything and Stan Cullis was enraged enough to storm away from what was really a friendly by offering waiting reporters a terse 'no comment'.

His temper was stoked by the sending-off in the 2-2 draw of Dave Woodfield just before half-time, with Wolves then ahead.

Wolverhampton, Bangu Bang Heads in Soccer

By ROY JUKICH

Wolverhampton 2, Bangu 2

Diplomatic soccer relations between Wolverhampton Wanderers of England and Bangu of Brazil are strained today.

The teams ignored the "exhibition" tag in Saturday night's international game at Empire Stadium and produced a bitterly-fought 2-2 draw. The Wolves had won six straight going into Saturday's game.

But the team's haven't seen the last of each other. They meet again Saturday in Toronto.

The Wolves are in Victoria tonight and return to Empire Stadium for a Wednesday game against the Vancouver All-Stars. Bangu is in Edmonton Wednesday.

The game was received with mixed emotions by the 20,148 fans and Wanderers' manager Stan Cullis. The two biggest pieces of conversation were the officiating of referee Frank Lee and the rugged checking of the Wolves.

Cullis, a former English International centre half, spent most of the night challenging Lee's calls and those by linesmen Reg Clark and Jim Miller. Miller and Clark didn't make Lee's job any easier.

Cullis' ranting became so embarrassing to Wolverhampton officials sitting in the Royal Box that vice-chairman J. R. Ireland was dispatched to the players bench to sit alongside the Wolves manager. It was only then that Cullis calmed down.

Cullis, however, barred the dressing room to visitors after the game and ordered his players not to talk to reporters. Cullis offered a terse "no comment" as he left the park.

Bangu Exploited Trouble

But it must also be noted that the Bangu players played on the sympathy of the referee and fans. They fell to the ground at the slightest contact.

For all their acting, the Brazilians knew their way around when it came to the infighting. Nilton Santos, for one, threw a few elbows and was given a wide berth toward the end.

The hard game played by Wolverhampton resulted in Dave Woodfield being ejected just before half time. Lee banished the centre half for

what he said was the deliberate kicking of Bianchini. This left the Englishmen to finish the game with 10 players. It marked the first time in 15 years that a member of a touring pro side has been tossed out here.

But despite the unpleasantness this night, the crowd was rewarded with an interesting and entertaining first half. The game deteriorated in the second half with Wolverhampton on the defensive and Bangu content to lay back and wait for the breaks despite the one-man advantage.

Broadbent Showed Class

Peter Broadbent and Chris Crowe were standouts for the Wolves. Broadbent, former English International, was the key figure in the attack and a defensive standout in the real half.

Crowe delighted the fans with his speed, ball control and ability to crack a ball with deadly accuracy. He scored the game's first goal at 21 minutes.

Jim Murray scored Wolves' second goal nine minutes later, snapping up Ted Farmer's rebound and catching the far corner.

Brazil's big break came at the 35 minutes when Lee called a penalty against George Showell for shoving. Pinto scored and Bangu came alive. Woodfield fouled Bianchini just before the half and from the resulting kick, Ramalho Beto tied the score at 2-2.

Chris Crowe looks on (left) and admires a header by Ted Farmer in a game watched by 19,339. Above: Terry Wharton about to feel the pain of a Bangu challenge.

Two photos that show why so many top English players played for Vancouver before they were done

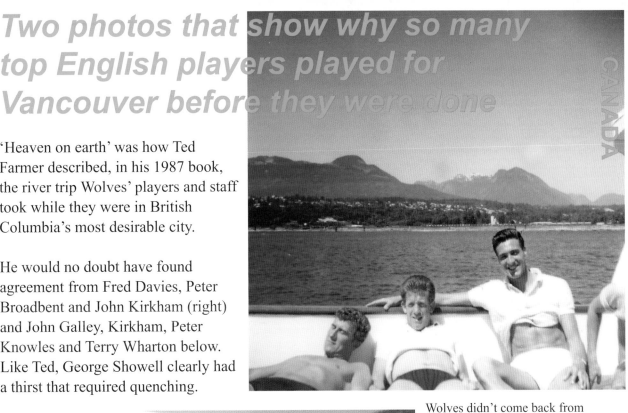

'Heaven on earth' was how Ted Farmer described, in his 1987 book, the river trip Wolves' players and staff took while they were in British Columbia's most desirable city.

He would no doubt have found agreement from Fred Davies, Peter Broadbent and John Kirkham (right) and John Galley, Kirkham, Peter Knowles and Terry Wharton below. Like Ted, George Showell clearly had a thirst that required quenching.

Wolves didn't come back from Canada with just sun tans and a host of victories. They also spotted the 15-year-old Les Wilson in a junior match and took him on after, at his father's insistence, he had finished his schooling. Wilson (below) was born in Manchester but raised in Vancouver and went on to be one of Wolves' most versatile players ever.

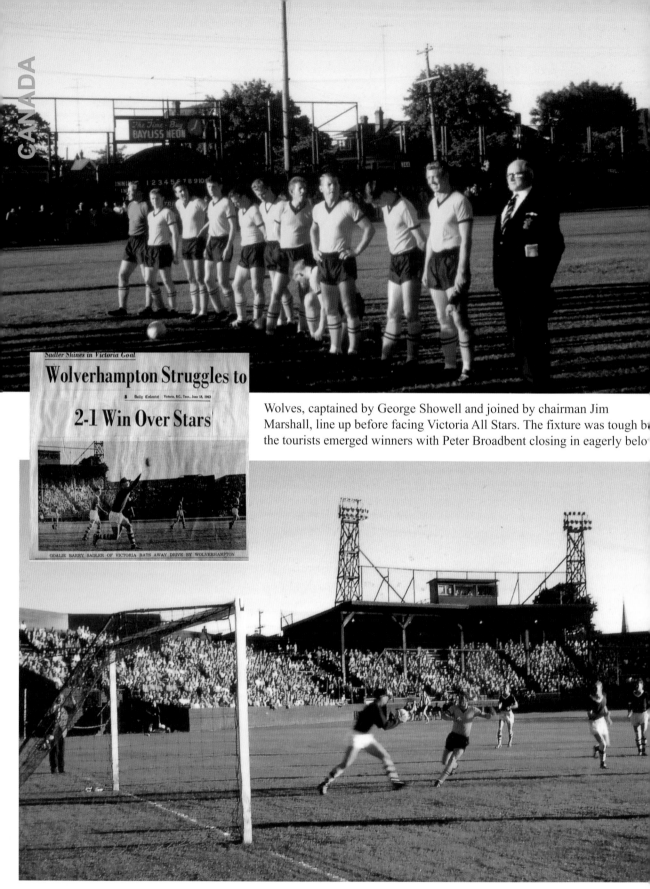

Sadler Shines in Victoria Goal

Wolverhampton Struggles to

8 **Daily Colonist** Victoria, B.C. Tues., June 18, 1963

2-1 Win Over Stars

GOALIE BARRY SADLER OF VICTORIA BATS AWAY DRIVE BY WOLVERHAMPTON

Wolves, captained by George Showell and joined by chairman Jim Marshall, line up before facing Victoria All Stars. The fixture was tough but the tourists emerged winners with Peter Broadbent closing in eagerly below

Johnny Hancocks had happy memories of Canada's bracing air. In the days when footballers often crossed the Atlantic by boat rather than air, frightened flier Johnny hit all his side's goals in a 4-4 1950 draw with Vancouver while playing for an FA XI. He also scored hat-tricks in Saskatchewan and Ontario on the America/Canada tour and totalled a staggering 16 goals in nine games.

Ted Farmer used the '63 tour to raise hopes that he could regain his best form after serious injury problems.

The no 9 stayed on the bench in the win over Victoria All Stars on Vancouver Island (above) but was back to net two against Vancouver All Stars and confirm himself as top tour marksman with 11 goals.

Taking in what was nearly their last look at the Pacific Ocean on tour as the Wolves party returned to the mainland from Vancouver Island were Ken Knighton, Peter Knowles and Terry Wharton. Following their 4-1 win over a Vancouver All Stars side back on the mainland, Stan Cullis's side headed across country and inland for their final game, which was to take place in Toronto.

THURSDAY, JUNE 20, 1963 PAGES 23 to 34 ***23

All-Stars Bright Enough To Impress Wanderers

Touring Englishmen Beat Vancouver, 4-1

By ROY JUKICH

Wolverhampton 4, Vancouver 1.

Vancouver All-Stars Wednesday lost the battle but won the war at Empire Stadium.

The All-Stars turned in a creditable performance before dropping a 4-1 exhibition soccer game to the touring Wolverhampton. It was a score before 13,664 fans. The win was the Wolves eighth against one tie in nine starts.

"Your team is the best outside of Bangu that we've met on our tour of North America," said Wanderers' manager Stan Cullis. "The fans here can be justly proud of them."

Cullis, at first, was reluctant to talk about any of the All-Stars. He later admitted Ken Pears and the half line of Bill Nicol, Bob Milo and Doug Greig played well.

Asked if any of the Wanderers played better than usual, Cullis replied: "I never openly make this type of observation."

Broadbent, Crowe Shine

"If I did, the players would accuse me of drinking and I don't drink."

But ask any of the All-Stars or the fans and they'd tell you Peter Broadbent and Chris Crowe were the standouts. Broadbent, English international, played another fine game.

Wolverhampton director W. C. Bpronon said, "Broadbent was out of this world."

"I've been watching Peter since he was 17," and Spronson," and have never seen him play better. He appeared to be enjoying himself every minute of the match."

Wolverhampton goalie Fred Davies wasn't exactly overworked but his save of Ken Varrior's drive late in the match was a masterpiece. He dove full length to send the drive against the upright, then recovered in time to clear.

PETER BROADBENT
...out of this world

ART HUGHES
Vancouver goalscorer

113

10,226 See Wolves Win Clever Game

By JOE TAYLOR

Wolverhampton Wanderers and Bangu of Brazil evidently left all their ill-feeling on the west coast. Saturday night's 4-1 triumph by the English first division side was a model of skill and decorum for the 10,226 fans at Varsity stadium.

This was in sharp contrast to a 2-2 tie by the same two teams a week ago. Vancouver papers described that outing as "more like war than soccer."

Harris clinched the decision after 15 minutes of the second half with a spanking shot from well out that hit the upright and stopped just on the line. Jim Murray helped it the rest of the way, but the goal went to Harris.

Wolves' keeper, Fred Davies, lost his own shutout when he dropped DeFelice's shot midway through the period, and Bianchini banged the loose ball into the net. To that point, Davies had been brilliant on the few oc-

Stobart wound up scoring at 30 minutes, on in a cross from Murray

Goal Line Gossip: W headed for home yeste sporting an unbeaten re in their 10-game tour. wins were Saturday's B decision, a 3-0 victory Mexico's B internationals a 4-2 triumph over Sch of West Germany. . . . will prove its real wort night when it meets Pre Munster of West Gern at Varsity stadium. The

Wolves ended their tour with a grudge match against Bangu, whose coach said: "We are from the country who are world champions and we must win." Both sides were better behaved and Barry Stobart netted two goals in a 4-1 win in which Farmer (seen above) and Gerry Harris also scored. Wolves had the support of British Navy personnel who stepped off two vessels in Toronto Harbour to don gold and black for the night. While in the area, Wolves visited Niagara Falls, as shown by this photo (right) of Messrs Cullis, Crowe, Galley, Knowles, Woodfield and Wharton.

THE PROVINCE, Friday, May 26, 1972

Aberdeen stars Alex Willoughby (left), Joe Harper flank Wolves goalie Phil Parkes.
—Gordon Sedawie photo

Four years and nine years later, having been to Division Two and back, Wolves returned to Canada.

Playing as Los Angeles Wolves in a lengthy 1967 tournament, they dropped in on Toronto to face and beat Scottish side Hibernian, Canadian-bred Les Wilson lining up in their victorious team.

Unfortunately for him, it was just after his departure to Bristol City that the club were next back in Canada; in his long-time home city to be precise. Vancouver was the venue for the third of a 1972 series of four games against Aberdeen, the club they famously beat in the final of the prestigious 1967 tournament in the United States. And they sent them packing again this time, 3-0 in front of almost 10,000 spectators that included Wilson and his wife.

True to form, the former Molineux utility man laid out the welcome mat for his old colleagues during their stay and gave one of them, Gerry Taylor, a guided tour of the city.

The other games on the 1972 trip were in the United States.

Jim McCalliog, seen (left) on the prowl in the 3-0 win over Aberdeen, had caught the eye at the Empire Stadium before. Near the end of a world tour with a Scotland side in 1967, he netted twice and Alex Ferguson once in a win over a Vancouver XI.

Wanderers blank Dons

By ROY JUKICH

Wolverhampton 3, Aberdeen 0.

Wolverhampton Wanderers ruled the soccer pitch Friday night at Empire Stadium.

Following a somewhat sluggish start, Wolverhampton put things together in a big way to blank Aberdeen 3-0 in last night's exhibition match before 9,165 fans. The victory was the Wolves' first in three tries against the Scottish side.

"That was by far our best effort of the tour," admitted Wanderers' manager Bill McGarry. "The pitch just suited us fine and our marksmanship was much improved over our previous appearances."

Wolverhampton's Ken Hibbitt and Hugh Curran treated the crowd to an excellent exhibition of shooting and never gave Aberdeen netminder Andy Geoghegan a moment's rest. Hibbitt possesses one of the hardest shots in British soccer today and on occasions Geoghegan was left gasping for air after blocking some of the howitzers.

The work of David Wagstaffe on the wings was also a treat to watch. Wagstaffe was allowed the freedom of the field and sent in crosses from the right and left wings with equal authority.

McGarry contends Wagstaffe is the best winger in Britain today and should be playing for England on a permanent basis. But he added, unfortunately, Sir Alf Ramsey (England's manager) doesn't play wingers.

Wolves goalie Phil Parkes also gave a pleasing exhibition in recording the shutout. He didn't have half the work of his counterpart but came through in sensational fashion in the second half.

Parkes' first big save was in the initial minute of the second half, going full length to steal the ball off the feet of James Forrest. Wolves, at the time, were leading 1-0 and

following the save marched down the field to make it 2-0.

David Robb, one of the few bright lights of a weak Aberdeen attack, and Ian Taylor also had a good crack at Parkes only to draw blanks. Robb almost broke the Wolves goalie in half with a bullet-like drive from close quarters while Taylor was robbed of a certain goal by a sprawling save after breaking in the clear.

Aberdeen manager Jimmy Bonthorne didn't offer any excuses for the defeat.

"We played badly," said Bonthorne, "and were punished for it. But there's always the next time."

The Dons' manager reluctantly admitted some of the players were hurting and shouldn't have played. "The players refused to disappoint the team's followers and insisted on having a go," he said.

Hibbitt scored the only goal of the opening half, going full length to head home Jim McCalliog's cross from the left side. Curran and Richards also had opportunities to add to Wolves' lead before the half.

John Richards made it 2-0 at five minutes on Hibbitt's rebound and Curran completed the scoring nine minutes later. Wagstaffe started the play on the right side with a smart cross.

It was also a great night for the B.C. Soccer Association Commission, back in the tour business after a four-year absence.

"I thought it was a good show," said Commission chairman Stu Ross, "and I think we'll show a small profit. We might even take another whack at a tour game. I said maybe, remember."

Wolves' feast

BY JEFF CROSS
Province Soccer Writer

Wolverhampton Wanderers of England had suffered enough already at the hands — and feet — of Scotland's Aberdeen.

So that when the two British soccer teams came together for a third time on their respective North American tours at Empire Stadium Friday night, there was the obvious matter of pride to be restored.

And the no nonsense Wolves made a fine job of the restoration, defeating the Scots 3-0 before a crowd announced as 9,165 in a game which rarely rose above its "exhibition" status.

The Wolves owed their success principally to a scheming, roaming will of the wisp named David Wagstaffe, with a sizeable assist from their giant goalkeeper Phil Parkes.

Wagstaffe wore number 11 on the back of his shirt, which in theory made him a left winger, but the spindly legged Waggy, as he is known in downtown Wolverhampton, used the whole playing pitch as his area of operation.

He set up two of the goals and generally had the Aberdeen defence falling over itself looking for him.

At the other end, goalie

Parkes, the six-foot-three bulwark of a man, dealt capably — at times bravely — with the few shots that the uninspired Scottish attack flung at him.

Two of them came in the space of a minute early in the second half.

The first was blocked when Parkes made a point blank save from David Robb, the second when the goalie dived daringly at the feet of Ian Taylor — then climbing to his feet thankful he had elected to play in track suit pants.

Parkes' opposite number, Andy Geoghegan, also wearing long pants against the possibility of burns from the artificial turf, did not have as happy a time.

With hesitant support in front of him, Geoghegan was often in trouble.

Wolves went ahead 1-0 at 26 minutes when Ken Hibbitt hurled himself horizontally to head in an accurate cross from Wagstaffe.

It was still 1-0 at halftime but not for much longer. Within five minutes of the restart, the hapless Geoghegan went to gather a shot from Hibbitt, only to drop it right at the feet of John Richards who swept it into the gaping net.

Then Wagstaffe set the scene for the third goal nine minutes later, with another great cross — this time from the right wing. Inside forward Alan Sunderland headed the ball towards goal where Geoghegan made a frantic lunge for it. He succeeded only in deflecting it into the path of the onrushing Hugh Curran who had only to guide it into the net.

The English team was on top of the Scots for almost all the evening in a game which often promised much, but came to life only in flashes — flashes provided mainly by Wagstaffe of the Wolves.

BRIEFLY . . . Two more interesting tour games are possible for Vancouver. Vancouver Spartans have permission to sponsor a tour by Hungary's Ferencvaros in August and Brazil's Santos, with Pele, could be here in July . . . Games here await the go-ahead from the B.C. Soccer Commission.

More soccer, Page 15

UNCLEAN....KEEP OUT!
Foot and mouth stopped Wolves in their tracks in 2001. They were due to go to Toronto for games as preparation for Dave Jones's first full season in charge but the trip was cancelled following the outbreak of the disease in the UK the previous winter.

USA

Shades of greatness

![Standard Stations Inc logo] We probably have more photos of Wolves in the USA than of their travels anywhere else on the globe. This is a long section but, as the inhabitants of this particular country might say: If you've got it, flaunt it!

Stan Cullis and chairman James Marshall decided against wearing flowers in their hair when they went on walkabouts among the unmistakable streets of San Francisco during Wolves' long 1963 summer tour.

Stan Cullis's squad saw plenty of airports during their demanding 1963 trip across the Atlantic and even refuelled at Prestwick in Scotland and Gander in Newfoundland en route. But, judging by their eye-care, George Showell, John Harris and Jimmy Murray (see facing page) had clearly heard a promising weather forecast.

Malcolm Finlayson, Johnny Kirkham, Harris and youngster John Galley are among those managing a perky stride across the tarmac (right) despite the tough travelling schedule.

Wolves had only two days on unfamiliar soil before the games began with a 5-1 win in Montreal. Then it was USA all the way for almost three weeks.

All smiles (well, nearly!) from the immaculately attired Terry Wharton, John Harris and Barry Stobart.

In the wake of 1950s trips to South Africa and Russia, the five-week trans-Atlantic adventure was another means of spreading Wolves' name across the globe. The Express & Star didn't go with them but photographed the tour party in their club blazers as they left Molineux early on Monday, May 20 – exactly a week after they finished the season in a healthy fifth place.

Five fixtures in America – two in New York and one each in Philadelphia, St Louis and San Francisco – were shoehorned in among five in Canada, with Wolves' squad impressed by the 'Big Apple'. There, they played at Downing Stadium on Randall's Island – a venue opened

almost 30 years earlier when Jesse Owens competed in a trial for the 1936 Olympics. The ground also hosted England's 10-0 victory over the USA in May, 1964, when Mike Bailey (then of Charlton) made his international debut alongside Bobby Thomson and Ron Flowers.

Thomson and Alan Hinton missed the 1963 tour as they were on international duty, both playing in an England under-23 victory over Yugoslavia in Belgrade in which the winger hit a hat-trick. That win came in between the second and third matches of Wolves' tour, which Flowers also missed as he was with his country's seniors.

Left: Malcolm Finlayson, George Showell, Gerry Harris, Fred Goodwin, Dave Woodfield, Johnny Kirkham and Chris Crowe go through the pre-match formalities while preparations take on a relaxed air in the photo at the top of the opposite page as Peter Broadbent, standing alongside Fred Davie, seems reluctant to put down his camera.

Opposite bottom: Ken Knighton, like John Galley a 'baby' of the trip at 19. Ted Farmer (left) was only 23 but top-scored on tour with his 11 goals. Below: Cullis, Bill Shorthouse, Knighton, Galley, Gerry Harris, Barry Stobart, Broadbent and Davies on the bench in New York.

In between their wins in New York over Schalke (4-2) and an American Soccer League XI (5-0), Wolves made the short hop south to Philadelphia to take on Ukrainian Nationals, who had won the Eastern Championship for the previous two years. The thermometer was rising and so was the tourists' goal tally as they emerged 3-2 victors in a competitive game.

With Bill Slater not on the trip as he prepared to call time on his long and illustrious career at Molineux, George Showell was tour skipper and is seen doing the pre-match honours above, with his manager offering moral support. Below (from left), Woodfield, Goodwin, Peter Knowles and Kirkham are the other players captured in this line-up.

Dear all.......working our socks off here, hardly a moment to ourselves. Will write again later, IF I get time.

Okay, we know Stan Cullis tolerated no let-up in standards and routine, even with so-called friendlies, so please permit us the rather tongue-in-cheek headline above.

As we have a number of photos from off-duty days and nights in America, we thought we would display them more light-heartedly.

Right: Messrs Kirkham, Broadbent, Harris (Gerry) and Showell let their hair down but who's the mischief-maker at the back? Below: Jimmy Murray and fellow marksman Ted Farmer in sociable mood.

At leisure (right) are Chris Crowe, Barry Stobart, Terry Wharton, Fred Davies, Dave Woodfield, John Galley and Peter Knowles.

Below: Fellow 'teens' Ken Knighton and John Galley in different modes of dress.

Opposite top: Who's in charge here? Stan meets his match!

Opposite bottom: Fred Davies, Jimmy Murray and Gerry Harris chat with a local official at one of many functions the players attended.

USA

INTERNATIONAL
SOCCER
BALBOA STADIUM

SUNDAY, JUNE 2, 1963
MEXICO CITY
SELECT
vs.
S. F. UNITED

SAN FRANCISCO

SUNDAY, JUNE 9,
ENGLAND'S
WOLVERHAMPTON
WANDERERS
vs.
S. F. UNITED

Wolves departed America with the record of five wins from five matches
after beating Mexican City Select 3-0 (above) in a game hastily arranged for San Francisco's Balboa

Stadium, a clash with a select XI having fallen through when terms could not be agreed.

Note where Wolves' players are standing for the national anthems before kick-off, which was performed by the lady dressed in red in the foreground – Miss San Francisco, Gale Dolores Heit.

Before entering the City by the Bay, Wolves also beat Catholic Youth Council 6-0 in St Louis, an old cutting (left) showing Ted Farmer challenging. Temperatures reached 98 in the Missouri capital, where Farmer, Stobart, Davies and Knighton spent a (planned!) day at the home of a senior detective in the city police.

The St Louis pitch came complete, near one touchline, with a long jump pit that had been kept for posterity as Ralph Boston broke the world record there. "From my central position, I watched both our wingers lose seven inches as they battled through the sand," Farmer said.

And, in 1967, the Wolves were back...

Above: Ronnie Allen and several of his players look on approvingly as Dave Burnside gives a keepy-uppy demonstration before the squad have even left the airport building. Below: Another hot one on match day.

The 1963 tour, as long as it was, was surpassed by the marathon jaunt under Ronnie Allen four years later in the aftermath of Wolves' wonderful Second Division promotion campaign.

No fewer than 14 matches, including one against their 1963 rivals Bangu, were played under the banner of Los Angeles Wolves in the United Soccer Association Championship – an ambitious tournament of over seven weeks that took in teams from Brazil, Italy, Holland and Uruguay as well as Northern Ireland, the Republic, Scotland and England.

GERALDINE CHAPLIN

Wolves clicked almost from the start of the 1967 adventure and were quickly pushing ha[rd] in the Western Division.

They had to overcome injuries, one or two disciplinary problems and even the need to throw Fred Davies on as an outfield player (left) against ADO Den Haag. The keeper put himself in the headlines by heading the killer second goal against the Dutchmen in LA.

As if criss-crossing the States and Canada for

THE LOS ANGELES WOLVES

There was gloom thicker than the proverbial English fog in Wolverhampton three seasons back. The famed Wolves (their actual nickname is Wanderers) had suffered the ignominy of relegation from England's major soccer league, the First Division, to the Second Division.

For the benefit of those unfamiliar with the system used in English soccer, two teams are demoted from the First Division each season and two are promoted from the Second Division as their replacements. For the Wolves, one of the oldest and proudest clubs in England, it was a shocker.

Ernie Hunt, inside right and one of the Wolves leading scorers.

No one knew how long it would take them to fight their way back into the ranks of the elite. The directors were determined to achieve this objective as quickly as possible. The time schedule was set at from three to five years. It took just two.

The advent of Ronnie Allen as manager and coach, and the solid support of Chairman John Ireland, the rest of the directors and the shareholders made this seeming miracle possible. Allen rebuilt the Wolves into a young, hard-tacking aggresive eleven that radiated team spirit. Some sagacious purchases, such as the $150,000 spent to acquire Derek Dougan, and the introduction of other new blood helped to produce a Wolves' team that quickly proved dynamic.

In the 1966-67, which concluded in early May, the Wolves led the Second Division practically until the final game of the season. Then, crippled by injuries, they went down to defeat and finished one point back of Coventry City. It was a disappointment, but at least they had realized their great ambition: The return to the First Division. And, as everybody agreed at the time, the Wolves are back where they belong.

When Jack Kent Cooke invited them to represent Los Angeles in the United Soccer Association, the Wolverhampton management jumped at the opportunity. "Not only will it be a wonderful reward for the lads for gaining promotion," Manager Allen commented, "but all that wonderful California sunshine will do them good."

When the Wolves met The Monkees

nearly two months wasn't exciting enough, flirting with the showbiz world added even more gloss.

Bobby Thomson was snapped with Charlie Chaplin's daughter Geraldine (opposite) and the players met actress Maureen O'Hara and British star Tommy Steele, who was starring in the film, The Happiest Millionaire. Also, Dave Wagstaffe's boyhood links in Manchester with Davy Jones led to more high life on tour – sampled by Waggy and Ernie Hunt (above) and the same duo plus Les Wilson, Graham Hawkins and Thomson (right). Below: Terry Wharton and Mike Bailey join Waggy and Ernie in getting to know Davy and his fellow Monkees better.

'No side could ever have had a better time on tour then we did in 1967' – Phil Parkes

Wolves' bronzed players were surprised to see their win over Den Haag – something of a revenge mission after a stormy defeat against the Dutch two days earlier – marked with a souvenir. From left, Gerry Taylor, Fred Davies, Paddy Buckley, Peter Knowles, Dave Woodfield and Ronnie Allen have a close-up above. Amid Wolves' superb progress, one venue proved more problematic....the dramatic Washington stadium (below), where they drew with Aberdeen, then lost in a re-match.

Never did Wolves deliver more brilliantly than in a dramatic final against Aberdeen, aka the Washington Whips, in the LA Coliseum (seen left).

Stamina and resilience were the key as they stayed strong to win a thrilling, epic match 6-5 on a golden goal that came when a cross by Bobby Thomson was turned into his own net by Ally Shewin.

UNITED SOCCER ASSOCIATION FINAL STANDINGS 1967

WESTERN DIVISION	W	L	T	Pts.	GF	GA	EASTERN DIVISION	W	L	T	Pts.	GF	GA
.A. WOLVES	5	2	5	15	21	14	Washington	5	2	5	15	19	11
an Francisco	5	4	3	13	25	19	Cleveland	5	3	4	14	19	13
hicago	3	2	7	13	20	14	Toronto	4	3	5	13	23	17
louston	4	4	4	12	19	18	Detroit	3	3	6	12	11	18
ancouver	3	4	5	11	20	28	New York	2	4	6	10	15	17
allas	3	6	3	9	14	23	Boston	2	7	3	7	12	26

One of the stories of the game, though, was the hat-trick by Frank Munro that played no small part in him becoming a Wolves player the following winter. The Scot was part of the joint lap of honour featuring John Holsgrove and Thomson below, with Derek Dougan playing the part of showman as usual by hurling his shirt into the 17,824 crowd. The no 9, also pictured right, scored once in a final that brought Dave Burnside a hat-trick as well. Doog had one moan, claiming in one of his books that he never received the camera he won in the USA when appearing on a lunchtime TV show!

Wolves were the tournament's second best supported team after Bangu (Houston Stars).

On to 1969.....some familiar faces

Greetings from

KANSAS CITY

25¢

MISSOURI

"HEART OF AMERICA"

UNION STATION AND SKYLINE

Wolves – still in British hands despite a bid from their popular LA franchise owner Jack Kent Cooke – entered another lengthy USA tournament when playing out of Kansas City throughout the month of May, 1969.

This time, all eight of their games were against British sides, namely West Ham, Dundee United, Kilmarnock and Aston Villa. Two of the matches were put back because of rain and, in a tournament in which extra points were awarded for goals, Wolves took a heavy toll on an Aston Villa squad by now containing Peter Broadbent and managed by Tommy Docherty.

Top: John Holsgrove and Les Wilson about to jet off back over the Atlantic. Right: The Kansas stadium Wolves grew to know well.

Derek Dougan scored a spectacular winner in Atlanta in the first clash against one of his former clubs after joining up late following Home International duty. For Northern Ireland, he played alongside one-time Wolves youngster Dave Clements – a highly successful businessman in much more recent times in America.

As in 1967, Wolves' players became popular residents and were not only introduced to Kansas City dignitaries at the Mayor's Parlour but also presented with illuminated scrolls designating them as honorary citizens. Manager Bill McGarry, chairman John Ireland and fellow director Jim Marshall received miniature keys to the city.

The warm welcome had begun on touchdown when they were greeted at the airport by 60 cheerleaders in red and white uniforms, with green mittens. But there was an inconvenience for Dave Wagstaffe when it was learned that his luggage had been sent instead to Las Vegas. His cases turned up two days after that of his team-mates.

Top: Wolves' players, back in black shorts, rather than the gold ones they had worn for several years, get ready for the formalities before kick-off. Right: Proof of how they were taken to the hearts of a city.

Smiles from Derek Clarke, Les Wilson, John McAlle, Peter Knowles, John Holsgrove and Frank Munro. Below: Action v West Ham.

HIT OR MISS
Marcus Hahnemann – not a bad torch-bearer as Wolves' first American signing. The keeper gave two fine Premier League years' service at Molineux. Yanks a lot!

Wolves opened with a defeat against West Ham in Baltimore but turned the tables by beating them 4-2 in Kansas a few days after defeating Dundee by the same score there.

John McAlle scored two goals at the right end and one at the wrong end in the win over the Hammers and was named as the Kansas City supporters' player of the tournament. Also important to him were the words of Peter Knowles, another regular scorer on the trip. The defender recalled: "It was during that tournament that Peter said to me: 'I didn't realise you were such a good player.'"

The 1969 competition was played more in the centre and eastern states of the country, with St Louis – also visited by Wolves in 1963 – and Dallas on their schedule as well.

In Baltimore, Mike Bailey met his former Charlton team-mate Gordon Jago – then boss of Baltimore Bays.

Wolves squeezed in a drawn friendly with Kansas City Spurs (above) but only ten players are in view. Peter Knowles, less than four months from quitting the game, did not 'do' national anthems. Plans for a game in Boston were scrapped at short notice, with America underwhelmed by 'soccer' when compared with news events. Neil Armstrong's momentous moon walk was only a few weeks away.

Happy as he was to return with the 3ft-high trophy (top right), McGarry wasn't sure football in the States – unlike the historic Apollo 11 mission – would take off. He felt the tour was too long and said: "The Americans had no idea about English football."

The USA trip in 1972 was short by comparison, Wolves playing four matches against Aberdeen, the club they had beaten in the 1967 final. In order, San Francisco, Seattle and Los Angeles were the American venues used, with the third game squeezed in over the border in Vancouver.

The outcome of the first game was no surprise, Wolves having a 20-hour journey shortly before while Aberdeen arrived via five days in Bermuda. Jim McCalliog scored first in the 3-1 loss at the Kezar

WOLVES — ABERDEEN RETURN TO LOS ANGELES

INTERNATIONAL SOCCER

LOS ANGELES COLISEUM

ENGLAND'S
FAMOUS "WOLVES"
WOLVERHAMPTON F.C.
versus
SCOTLAND'S
DYNAMIC "DONS"
ABERDEEN F.C.

SUNDAY MAY 28 3:00 P.M.

OUTSTANDING PRELIMINARY GAMES
AT 11:00 A.M. and 1:00 P.M.
JUNIOR ALL-STARS — (12 to 15) — 16 to 19)
LOS ANGELES versus SAN FRANCISCO

POPULAR PRICES:
In Advance . . . . $4.50   Day of the game $5.00
Juniors in Advance . . . . . . $1.00   Day of the game $2.00

Stadium and the Scots then won 3-0 at Seattle's High School Memorial Stadium on an artificial surface.

Wolves won the other games clearly, though, a John Richards hat-trick and a goal by Frank Munro making it a happy return to the LA Coliseum, with another trophy to show as a result (right).

The club went back to the US under John Barnwell in 1981 (left) and lost a one-off friendly 4-1 despite a Richards goal.

KICK
May 16, 1981
GATOR BOWL

SPECIAL EDITION

Wolverhampton Wanderers

VS.

Jacksonville Tea Men

FIRST EVER INTERNATIONAL SOCCER MATCH IN JACKSONVILLE

133

WEST INDIES

Well, it beats going to Portsmouth or Stoke

Long before 'conscription' was introduced for cricket's Barmy Army and sports-orientated travel to the Caribbean became relatively commonplace as a result, Wolves jetted away to the sun-kissed islands on a jaunt that will surely never be repeated.

As if a 43-game domestic season wasn't sapping enough, Stan Cullis had his players packing their bags a fortnight or so later for a unique eight-match stay.

Their island-hopping around Barbados, Trinidad and Jamaica – all locations more familiar with lovers of cricket – must have been interesting enough. Add on a few days in Haiti and this really did become a tour with a difference.

Top: Tour skipper Jimmy Melia carries out the pre-match duties with Sir John Stow, Governor of Barbados, just over half a century ago. Right: A striker alone in his thoughts.....Ray Crawford catches some sun in between games.

Is that what passed for a subs' bench in the Windies? Peter Broadbent plays up to the camera alongside Graham Hawkins and Jim Barron - the two men who formed Wolves' management team almost 20 years later. The photo below shows a pre-match line-up, with Melia and a half-hidden Davies nearest the camera. Beyond them are Le Flem, Woodfield, Wharton, Knowles, Woodruff, Stobart, Crawford, Hawkins, Crowe, Barron and Showell. Right: A souvenir from the tour.

Wolves v Chelsea - but it's nothing like Molineux or Stamford Bridge

A long way from West London and the West Midlands, Chelsea and Wolves prepare to battle it out in the West Indies instead. Lining up under a hot Barbados sun are a mixture of players from the two clubs. Back row, from left: John Dunn, Graham Hawkins, Tommy Docherty, Ron Harris, George Showell, Jim Barron, Marvin Hinton, Terry Venables, David Woodfield, John Mortimore, Dick Le Flem, Fred Davies, Ian Watson, Peter Broadbent, Gerry Harris, John Kirkham, Ray Crawford. Front: Alan Harris, Chris Crowe, Barry Bridges, Bobby Woodruff, Eddie McCreadie, Peter Knowles, Jimmy Melia, Barry Stobart and John Hollins.

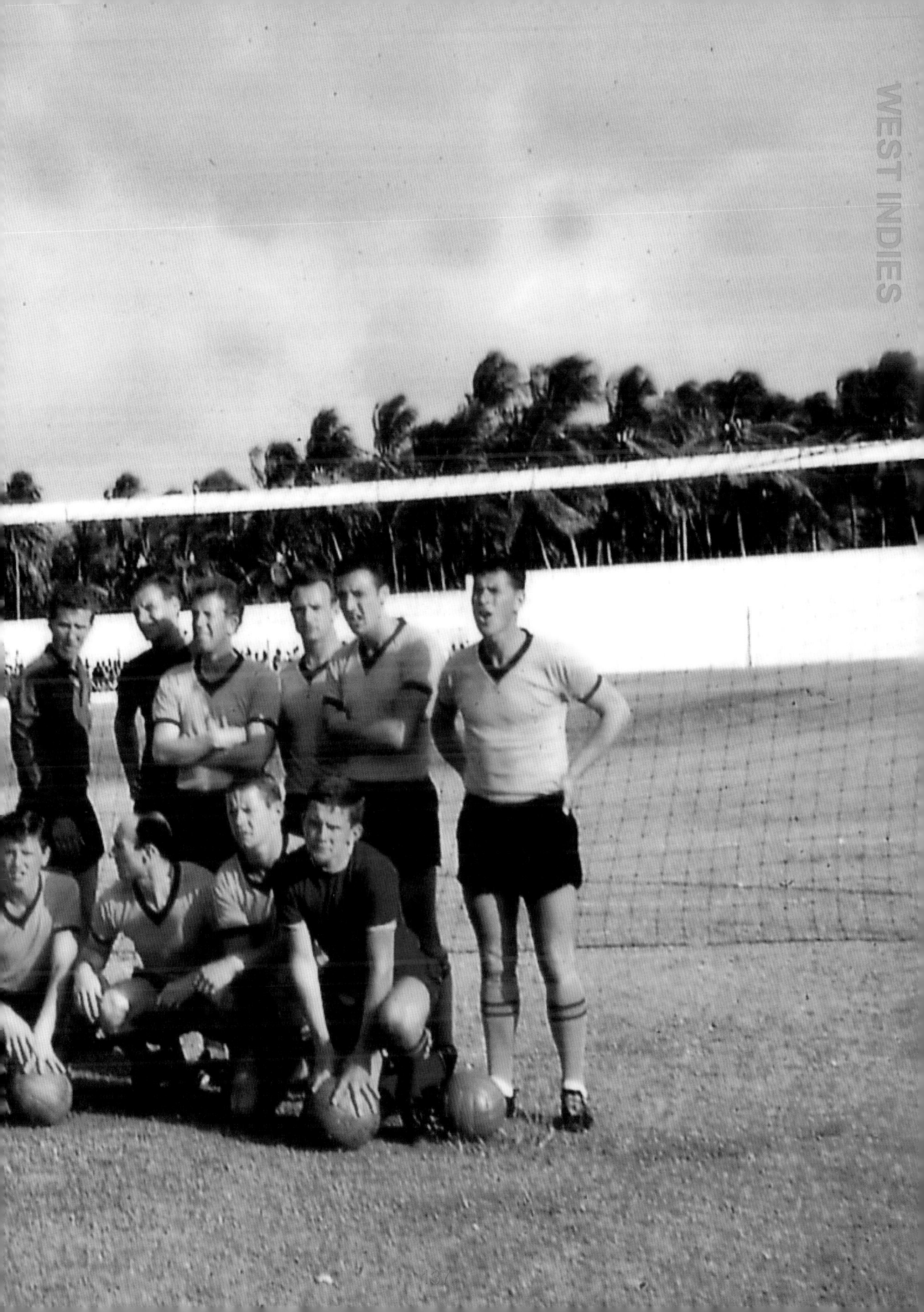

Five of Wolves' eight games on tour were against Chelsea, the first at the Kensington Oval cricket ground in Barbados on May 21 bringing them a 3-1 win the day after the Londoners had beaten an island XI 7-0. Dick Le Flem sensationally opened the scoring from 30 yards in the first minute and, although Barry Bridges equalised in the 27th minute, two goals by Ray Crawford settled the first of what were described as exhibition matches between the clubs.

Chelsea, beaten home and away by Wolves in 1963-64, included Tommy Docherty in their side in the first half and had his coach Dave Sexton lining up for them in the second.

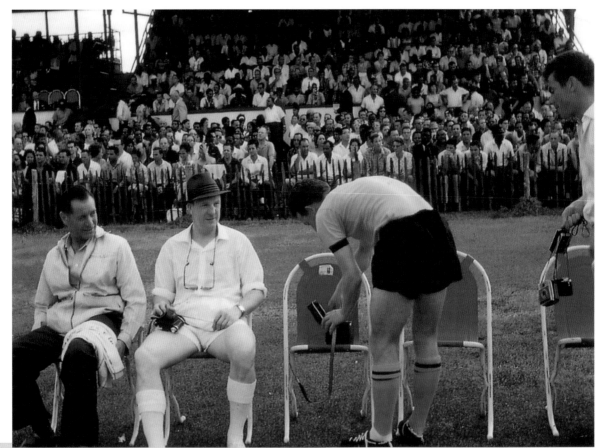

Stan Cullis would presumably have torn a strip off his players at many other times if he ever thought they were behaving like tourists. Here, though, relaxed and looking very much like the Englishman abroad with his trusty right-hand man Joe Gardiner at his side, he smiles as Peter Broadbent puts down his camera after use. The other player creeping into shot is winger Dick Le Flem. Left: Ray Crawford scores one of his two goals in the 3-1 victory over Chelsea in Barbados.

As the travelling show moved south, some 30 miles from the South America mainland, Wolves thrashed Trinidad 4-0 thanks to Crawford's hat-trick but the Londoners hit back in the series when they beat their Division One rivals 3-2 in Port of Spain in pouring rain the following night. All the goals came in the second half, with Terry Venables scoring a late winner from a penalty conceded by Gerry Harris.

The 25,000 crowd were witnesses to an unusual event after John Dunn was injured diving at Crawford's feet. With Peter Bonetti nursing a temperature, Wolves agreed to let keeper Jim Barron swap sides for the rest of the game. He obviously did well, too, because he subsequently joined the Londoners permanently.

Two of the modes of dress on tour, as shown off above by Graham Hawkins and below by (from left) Dick Le Flem, Peter Knowles, Ray Crawford and Dave Woodfield. The trip must have been hard for Woodfield, who had married just a week before the players flew out.

THE WEST INDIAN TOBACCO CO. LTD.

FOOTBALL FESTIVAL

THE WEST INDIAN TOBACCO COMPANY LIMITED

Arranged through the courtesy of
The Trinidad Football Association

VISIT OF CHELSEA AND
WOLVERHAMPTON WANDERERS FOOTBALL
CLUBS TO TRINIDAD
MAY 1964

Matches were described as 'full-blooded', although the pace did sometimes drop in the heat and with the fatigue that came with meeting each other five times in only 17 days. On top of that punishing schedule, there was the extra tiredness that came from the succession of internal flights.

CITY OF PORT OF SPAIN

RECEPTION

in honour of

The Visiting Wolverhampton and Chelsea
Football Teams of England

at the

Auditorium, Town Hall

on

Friday 22nd May, 1964.

Top: A pitch of invasion of the acceptable kind in Port of Spain. Above: A keepsake from some socialising. Left: Relaxation time, with Dave Woodfield and Bobby Woodruff in the foreground and Jim Barron, John Kirkham, Peter Broadbent and Peter Knowles among those in the background.

Competitive but good mates off the field

Many years later, Peter Bonetti, his boss Tommy Docherty and the coach Frank Upton all pitched up at Wolves in managerial or coaching roles.

And there might have been one other transfer of personnel had The Doc had his way, Wolves centre-forward Ray Crawford revealing in his autobiography that he was sounded out by the manager over cocktails in a hotel during the trip. Such encounters were certainly possible. The two squads jostled for the best sun-loungers round the pool, shared flights and buses and saw more than enough of each other on the pitch. As these two photos above show, the fraternisation came naturally, with Chris Crowe having a joke at the expense of Alan Harris that is fully appreciated (above left) by Barry Stobart and Peter Knowles while George Showell took a dip (above right) among a group of Chelsea players including Terry Venables (foreground) and Eddie McCreadie. Below: Wolves' squad line up in Bridgetown.

Forget football, we're having a day out.....an idea that brought full approval from (left to right) Johnny Kirkham, George Showell, Jim Barron, Terry Wharton, Bobby Woodruff, Peter Broadbent and their guide.

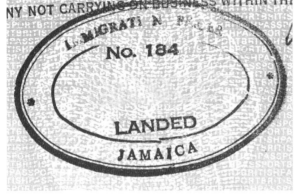

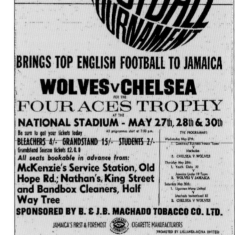

Wolves cut loose in Jamaica as they made it two victories out of three against Chelsea with a 4-2 success in the National Stadium that included a brace from Crawford and a Frank Upton own goal. A 13,000 crowd were present for the game, which was played on the same day that Mike Bailey (then of Charlton) made his England debut in a 10-0 win over the USA in New York in which Bobby Thomson and Ron Flowers also played.

Forty-eight hours later came an 8-4 romp for Wolves over Jamaica in the capital, Kingston. Alas, they then lost 3-0 in another game with Chelsea, who received a 2ft silver trophy from Prime Minister Donald Sangster for winning the two-game series on the island on aggregate.

At the time, cricket was much more popular in the Caribbean than football. When Wolves set foot on the Kensington Oval in Bridgetown, Barbados, they were treading the turf on which Geoff Boycott and John Edrich would have to go out and take guard against the fearsome West Indies opening attack of Wes Hall and Charlie Griffith on England's next tour there in 1967-68. That must have been even tougher than facing an irate Stan Cullis......

HIT OR MISS

Floyd Streete – one stylish, cool and popular dude.

Jason Roberts – should have been a big hit but his tally of caps with Grenada (five) was five more than the number of games he played for Wolves.

As well as big Floyd, Jamaica gave us Bob Hazell and 1970s reserve midfielder Don Gardner.

Left: Dick Le Flem gives chase along with a Chelsea defender clad unusually in all white. Above: Barry Stobart in his smart club gear. Top left: Time for self-composure during the pre-match formalities for (from left) Woodruff, Kirkham, Knowles, Wharton, Woodfield and Le Flem.

Blackpool-based Ken Parr (seen above with his linesmen) secured himself a nice month's work when appointed to trail round the Caribbean and officiate at all the Wolves-Chelsea games. And there was an interesting follow-up.

He was in the crowd at Bloomfield Road at the end of the following season when a Chelsea side destined to finish third in the top flight were the visitors. Parr had by then had to retire from regular refereeing because of a back problem but was trusted enough by Tommy Docherty to be accepted on to the field for a short stint in emergency when the match-night ref was injured.

Terry Wharton has never forgotten the '64 trip. First, he cut his foot when kicking out in panic and hitting a metal part of his bed after his room-mate John Kirkham jumped on him while having a nightmare. Having had stitches, the winger had nearly recovered when Stan Cullis, sat next to him, got over-involved in the action, swung his foot while watching a game and reopened his no 7's wound. Finally, Wharton sustained a black eye that was serious enough for a hospital visit when he suffered a clash of heads in scoring against Haiti.

Left: The bodies beautiful, as displayed by (from left) messrs Barron, Knowles, Harris, Hawkins, Stobart and Davies.

44

Stan Cullis (seen above earlier in the tour) was close to the end at Wolves as farewells were said to the Caribbean with a 1-1 draw against Haiti in rain-lashed Port Au Prince and a 2-0 defeat by Chelsea two nights later. The two clubs were probably ready for a good break from each other but, incredibly, with sun tans topped up by the less reliable English summer, they were pitched together at Molineux on the first day of the following season by the fixture planners. Chelsea won 3-0 and the legendary boss was gone three weeks later, with The Doc (shown below just before boarding) staying at Stamford Bridge until 1967.

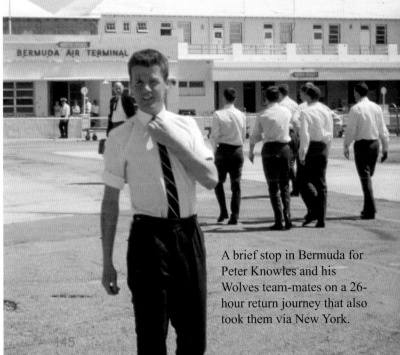

A brief stop in Bermuda for Peter Knowles and his Wolves team-mates on a 26-hour return journey that also took them via New York.

YUGOSLAVIA

Wolves' trip to the fringes of Eastern Europe four and a half decades ago might be viewed as another of those 'did they really need it?' tours. The squad had been on long, successful treks round the United States in two of the previous three summers and approached the close season of 1970 virtually on their knees, having ended their First Division campaign with four straight defeats and a 13-game win-less run.

Any thoughts that the players might be given a proper break, though, were brushed aside by the daunting schedule Bill McGarry had lined up – three games on tour of Yugoslavia, then four in the Anglo Italian Cup.

Dave Wagstaffe and Mike O'Grady were ruled out of the tour in the Balkans by injury and

Wolves players and officials, with locals, at an Embassy function in Yugoslavia. From left to right, irrespective of whatever level they are stood at, are: John McAlle, Derek Clarke, Paul Walker (half hidden), Dave Maclaren, Mike Bailey, John Ireland, Les Wilson, Kenny Hibbitt, Bill McGarry, John Richards, Dave Woodfield, Frank Munro, Derek Parkin, John Oldfield, Jim McCalliog, John Holsgrove.

Gerry Taylor enjoying some of the local hospitality.

Derek Dougan and Bertie Lutton because of Northern Ireland commitments, and those four may have had a chuckle when hearing that their team-mates had encountered snow when touching down.

The side nevertheless became the first overseas visitors in 25 years to defeat Zeljeznicar Sarajevo, only to then lose comfortably to both Sloboda and Skopje.

Wolves' resources were so severely stretched for the final fixture that coach Sammy Chung had to go on as a substitute. But there was a context to their 5-2 defeat. Monuments to the 1,000 Skopje citizens killed in an earthquake seven years earlier left a deep impression on many of the players.

HIT OR MISS
Nenad Milijas – the fact the Serbian helped Wolves survive in the Premier League and scored some spectacular goals makes him more hit than miss.

The club's only previous trip to Yugoslavia before 1970 had been a happier affair. A Norman Deeley goal earned them a 1-1 draw against Red Star Belgrade in the first round of the 1959-60 European Cup and they built on the performance by winning the return at Molineux easily. The front page of the programme and the team-line-ups, bewildering as they may be, are seen here.

High kicking from John Richards in Wolves' superb UEFA Cup quarter-final draw against mighty Juventus in Turin in 1971-72.

Wolves never visited Italy during their glory years – and it seems surprising they went to America, Canada and the Caribbean first. But they proved themselves a good fit for the famous boot when they did finally drop in.

The Anglo Italian Cup was the cue for their first trip in spring, 1970, a week or two after their three-match tour of Yugoslavia. In this new tournament, teams played four group games – two at home against clubs from the other country and two away versus the same opponents, with an extra point awarded for each goal scored.

Bill McGarry's side, having suffered a dreadful end to the Division One campaign, were well placed after two odd-goal victories at Molineux and topped their group when a 3-1 win in Florence brought them five points on the day John Richards scored his first senior goal.

That victory over Fiorentina was something of a triumph over adversity. Their promised access to a stadium in the resort of Viareggio didn't materialise because of a stoppage involving municipal workers, so Wolves had to travel another six miles to a village stadium in Forte del Marmi to train. And they squeezed in a little-known friendly in between their two AIC assignments when they beat Forte del Marmi 3-0 with goals by Derek Dougan (2) and Hugh Curran.

Industrial trouble was also in the air in the Italian capital. Just before Wolves' game against Lazio, the Roma v Middlesbrough clash was put back two days because of a strike by employees of the Italian Olympic Committee.

The congested tournament schedule meant Sunderland and Albion, as well as McGarry's men, were due to play at the Olympic Stadium (see photo opposite bottom) in the space of a few days. And Wolves' visit was made an unhappy one when they lost 2-0 before a 43,000 crowd. That put paid to their challenge in a competition which wasn't without its controversy. Dave Wagstaffe was twice booked at home to Lazio but for some reason not sent off – and the visitors had Giorgio Chinaglia dismissed by the Italian referee, Signor Carminatti.

Leicester's Gordon Hill officiated the return and issued marching orders to home keeper Sulfaro in a bust-up that appeared to be the 'afters' from an ill-tempered first leg.

| pagina 6 | CALCIO | Corriere dello Sport |

ANGLO-ITALIANO

Lazio-Wolverhampton 2-0 (1-0)

LAZIO: Sulfaro; Wilson, Facco; Governato, Papadopulo, Marchesi; Massa, Mazzola, Ghio, Nanni, Chinaglia; portiere di riserva: Di Vincenzo; Tomy, Oddi. (All.: Lorenzo).

WOLVERHAMPTON WANDERERS: Parkes; Taylor, Parkin; Bailey, Holesgrove; Richards, Walker (Shaw dal 29' della ripresa), Curran (Latton al 18' della ripresa), Wagstaffe; portiere di riserva: Oldfield; Shaw, McAlle, Latton. (All.: McGarry).

ARBITRO: Hill (G.B.).
MARCATORI: nel primo tempo al 41' Ghio; nella ripresa al 18' Ghio.

NOTE; serata primaverile, terreno in discrete condizioni, Spettatori 30 mila circa dei quali 23 mila 661 paganti per un incasso di 32 milioni 855.200. Al 38' della ripresa l'arbitro su segnalazione del guardalinee espelleva dal campo Sulfaro per un fallo di reazione su Latton. Calci d'angolo 6-1 per il Wolverhampton (5-1 nel primo tempo).

Ghio segna nella ripresa il secondo gol biancazzurro

The heat was on in another way when the club next played in Italy – in the 1971-72 UEFA Cup. Victories over opponents from Portugal, Holland and East Germany were small beer compared with the task that awaited McGarry's men against Juventus – Helmut Haller, Pietro Anastasi, Fabio Capello and all – in the quarter-final.

But Wolves played brilliantly to pull off

a 1-1 draw in the first leg at the Stadio Communale. "It was the best game we ever played," said Frank Munro, a memorable 2-1 victory in the second leg back at Molineux completing the task against the 2015 Champions League finalists on a night which left the victorious players with dubious memories of the behaviour of Capello. There were recollections of a fonder nature from the presence of the legendary John Charles, who accompanied Wolves' squad on their Turin trip and was feted wherever he went as a result of his time in Italy. 'Signor Charlo' is seen above on the bench with McGarry and injured skipper Mike Bailey, who described him as 'my idol'.

Much-missed Wolves fan Jim Heath, then a young boy, used a clever ploy to talk his father, who wasn't a fan, into letting him go to Juventus – he let him think it was the home leg! Jim's itinerary and match ticket are seen here, with the photo left showing the handsome gift the Italians presented to Wolves.

The combat was lower-key when the club returned to the Anglo Italian Cup more than two decades later. Having failed to qualify through the domestic phase in 1992-93 and 1993-94, they twice went travelling in 1994-95 after the format had been changed for Graham Taylor's first and only full season in charge. A hot late-August trip to the heel of Italy's boot took them to Lecce (above), not far from where Stan Cullis and Matt Busby had met while coaching the troops during the war.

David Kelly's goal secured victory but the club's interest in the competition was waning after a home defeat to Ascoli by the time they visited Venezia in early October (photo below). The attendance of 750 is said to be the smallest Wolves have ever played a competitive senior game in front of and a shadow side were beaten more easily than the 2-1 scoreline suggests.

The trip still had its highlights. Fans travelled to and from the island-based stadium by ferry and some of the Wolves party journeyed back to their hotel afterwards by speedboat.

MALTA

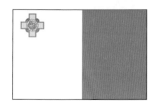

'Frequent fliers' is a tag that applied very aptly to Wolverhampton Wanderers around the time they landed on this sunshine island 44 years ago. Israel, Greece and Belgium were other destinations for one-off games around the same time but a four-day stay in the coastal resort of Sliema was a welcome tonic for the players, falling as it did between First Division games against Leeds and Liverpool in February, 1971.

Wolves trained in the match stadium in Gzira twice before their 5-1 demolition of Marsa, who actually equalised from a penalty mid-way through the second half. John Holsgrove's header forced the own goal that restored the lead on an afternoon on which Derek Dougan, Jimmy McCalliog and Hugh Curran were looking on, injured.

Bill McGarry's hand was further weakened as the Malta trip clashed with the second leg of an FA Youth Cup semi-final against West Ham. That tie robbed him of the services of Steve Daley, Alan Sunderland and Peter Eastoe but Wolves still had more than enough about them.

Top: Wolves attack through an airborne John McAlle. Left: Bobby Gould flashes in the opening goal and the first of his two in the 5-1 victory. Above: The home defence find themselves under further threat in what was then the national stadium - note the unusual sandy surface and patterned woodwork. Malta-based Wolves fans were delighted by the appearance of these cutting-edge colour photos, which are taken from the front page of their press. Back home, McGarry's men showed that the travelling didn't harm them as they beat Liverpool with a goal by Mike O'Grady.

The club have quite a following on the island, as underlined by the presence of the Malta Wolves Supporters Club, many of whose members still make at least one trip a season to Molineux.

Alfred Camilleri, pictured in tie left with Derek Dougan when the striker was ruled out of the 1971 clash, is the club's long-time president as well as being a fan for around 60 years. He was eager to attend the party (below) along with the likes of John Holsgrove, Hugh Curran, Doog, Sammy Chung, the two-goal Bobby Gould and Mike O'Grady and also welcomed Ron Flowers to a supporters' gathering around the same time during the England man's family holiday (bottom photo).

Alan Sunderland has settled in Malta and acted as interpreter when his former Molineux team-mate Barry Powell took Abersytwyth there for an Inter Toto Cup tie against Floriana. "We had a great time and I asked him to do a bit of scouting," Powell said. "But I think he watched the wrong team."

Derek Parkin's closest flirtation with a senior cap came when he was named by England for a Euro qualifier in Malta in February, 1971. But he stayed on the bench and then missed the club trip to the island three weeks later because he and Frank Munro were on opposite sides for the Scotland v England under-23 international in Glasgow.

The Malta fans saw their favourites again in 1985 (above), albeit in a time of deep gloom after the second of the club's nightmare three successive relegations. The trip was not official and proved a swansong for boss Tommy Docherty, who arrived after the opening victory over Xewkija Tigers on the neighbouring island of Gozo and returned early, as did a Charlton-bound John Humphrey (see photo right).

A follow-up game against a Gozo and Maltese Select XI brought an emphatic win and Wolves were due to face the country's champions once the deciding clash between Rabat and Hamrun had been played. But neither opponents came forward and the Third Division new arrivals had more familiar foes to tackle in the form of Shrewsbury, who proved too strong for them by winning 5-2 in Marsa back on the main island. That game was played in aid of the families of the Bradford Fire Disaster victims, the tragedy having occured a few days earlier. Coach Sammy Chapman's son Campbell was one of the losers' scorers.

Twenty-five years after Derek Parkin, another Wolves full-back had more luck. Ryan Green was 17 years and 226 days old when ex-Molineux favourite Bobby Gould saw to it that he replaced a better known Ryan G as the youngest senior Welsh international of all time by selecting him for the country's 3-0 friendly win in Malta in June, 1998. Remarkably, it was Green's first game in professional first-team football.

JERSEY

Two trips to Jersey, eight years apart, have brought Wolves two 9-0 victories. But the second of those wins came very much under the radar.

When John Barnwell's squad of League Cup winners made the hop to the Channel Islands at the end of 1979-80, the goal avalanche went unreported here. Even John Richards' Express & Star column overlooked the game against Jersey's under-23s and referred only to training sessions on the beach and to John McAlle being delegated as 'go to' man whenever the ball ended in the sea.

Jersey-based Wolves fan Stan Journeaux has enabled us to fill in this hole in the record books.....

Rising to the occasion: Andy Gray, Wolves' Scottish international, gets high to demonstrate his power in the air

League Cup holders score nine at Springfield

Soccer Wolves style!

Jersey Under 23s 0, Wolverhampton Wanderers 9

The 1980 game was played in front of around 3,000 at the Springfield Stadium in the capital St Helier on May 6.

From these Jersey Post cuttings Stan kindly sent us, we learned that Wembley hero Andy Gray required only a few seconds to volley in the first of the six goals Wolves rattled in during the first half.

After half-time, Kenny Hibbitt and Gray added further goals before the finishing flourish came from skipper Emlyn Hughes, who was still in celebration mode when a pitch invasion by hundreds of fans prompted the referee to signal an end to the slaughter several minutes early.

As the various items of Molineux-based literature don't carry any details of the game, we are happy to go the extra mile in this section by listing John Richards, Mel Eves, George Berry, Peter Daniel and Derek Parkin as the other marksmen and naming the team as: Kearns; Palmer, Berry, Hughes, Parkin; Hibbitt, Brazier, Daniel, Eves; Richards, Gray.

Willie Carr and Paul Bradshaw were absent nursing injuries before the club finished their season with home matches against Arsenal and Nottingham Forest.

Emlyn Hughes leads Wolves out in St Helier, followed by Colin Brazier and Derek Parkin. Below: Andy Gray in action in the game, six weeks on from his famous Wembley winner.

The weather was nothing like as accommodating when Wolves visited Jersey in late January, 1972. On a bitter night at the same venue, they defied the conditions by giving Jersey Wanderers a football lesson on the occasion of the host club's 75th anniversary.

But the locals faced an anxious wait following Wolves' touchdown from Birmingham, with Bill McGarry giving the pitch a long inspection before declaring he was happy for the game to go ahead.

His side were three up by the time they loaned Danny Hegan and Hugh Curran to the island champions. It was still one-sided, though, with Jim McCalliog's four goals leading the way. The Scot was one of the few Wolves men who had visited Jersey before.

Phil Parkes wore tracksuit bottoms to reduce the risk of injury and his counterpart wished he had done likewise after he and Derek Dougan went off after a painful landing. Not that the home keeper was extended when Kenny Hibbitt unexpectedly blazed a penalty over.

Amid few of the privacy worries that would exist

JERSEY EVENING POST, TUESDAY, FEBRUARY 1, 1972

DEREK DOUGAN (No. 10) sees this header scrambled away by the Wanderers' defenders

FOOTBALL

JERSEY WANDERERS 0,
WOLVERHAMPTON WANDERERS 9

WOLVES' SHARPSHOOTERS HIT NINE AGAINST MARQUIS CHAMPIONS

1,700 spectators shiver at Springfield

THE FAMED Wolves, four times FA Cup winners, three times First Division champions, and currently placed sixth in the fight for the premier title, delighted an approximate 1,700 crowd at Springfield yesterday evening with an exhibition of direct and skilful soccer.

report : BILL CUSTARD
REG CRIDLAND

Exchanges were keen and

JERSEY JOHN
John McAlle has become a frequent visitor back to the island.....his daughter has lived there in more recent years.

THE SADDEST OF NEWS
Pre-war Wolves keeper Alex Scott died suddenly on holiday in Jersey in August, 1973, at the age of only 59.

JERSEY WANDERERS F.C. versus
WOLVERHAMPTON WANDERERS F.C.

Monday, 31st JANUARY, 1972
SPRINGFIELD STADIUM Kick Off 7.30p.m.

SOUVENIR PROGRAMME 5p

today, the match programme announced that Wolves were staying near the airport at the Mermaid Hotel in St Peter – 'Jersey's most luxurious and modern hotel.' The building later became a residential home but was used by Wolves for changing because the dressing rooms at the ground didn't have adequate heating.

Jersey's proximity to France is illustrated by the fact the linesmen were named Le Breton and Roscouet and one of the home players was called Le Main.

Furthermore, the following day's banquet was held at the Hotel De France.

Wolves' trip had apparently cost £1,200 but did include 'island drives' and some golf. And they were following in distinguished footsteps as Manchester United had dropped in several weeks earlier.

Wolves' best-known other link with the Channel Islands is their signing of Guernsey-born Dick Le Flem in 1964. The former England under-23 international winger petered out after a bright start with the club, not helped by contracting jaundice during a summer back home.

Stan Journeaux, whose help with this section is greatly appreciated, tells us he was lucky enough to have been at Wembley for Billy Wright's 100th cap, for the 1974 and 1980 League Cup finals, the 1988 Sherpa Van Trophy final and for all of England's matches during the 1966 World Cup finals.

Above: John Richards takes aim at Springfield Stadium. Top left: A keepsake of Wolves' 1972 visit to Jersey.

ISRAEL

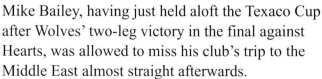

Mike Bailey, having just held aloft the Texaco Cup after Wolves' two-leg victory in the final against Hearts, was allowed to miss his club's trip to the Middle East almost straight afterwards.

His wife was about to give birth to their second child but Bill McGarry was nevertheless a happy man as he offered despatches by telephone to the Express & Star about a squad who were led instead by Jim McCalliog.

McGarry said of his side's 3-1 win over the national side in Tel Aviv: "It was a tremendous game, played to a full house. We really did play well." And his mood and platitudes stretched to where the squad were staying. "It's a glorious spot," he added. "The sunshine is beautiful."

Israel included nine of the players who had taken them to the World Cup finals in Mexico the previous year and were making a serious game of it when, following Derek Parkin's 25-yard drive for the opening goal, they equalised just past the hour.

But Paul Walker restored the lead with another long-range shot that went in off the bar and Bobby Gould tapped in a late third after Kenny Hibbitt was denied.

WOLVES WIN THRILLER

ISRAEL 1, WOLVERHAMPTON WANDERERS 3

The power and speed of English League soccer was good enough to give Wolverhampton Wanderers the edge in this four-goal thriller last night.

In a match before a jam-packed 22,000 crowd in Jaffa's Bloomfield Stadium — there were thousands locked outside — Wolves and the Israel national team contrived to put on a display that is unfortunately a rarity here.

The Israelis indeed played above themselves and it was good to see Hapoel Jerusalem's Eli Ben-Rimoj in superb form. It is an injustice that a player

minute. He slipped a pass to full-back Parkin coho smashed home a fierce shot into the corner from 30 yards.

It was still all-action as Wolves — with Curren and Hibbitt on for Dougan and O'Grady — fought to prevent Israel grabbing an equaliser.

But they were not successful. In the 64th minute Ben Rimoj fooled the whole defence. flicked the ball sideways — and winger George Borba smashed it home from six yards.

LAP OF HONOUR

Israel then began to make a bid for the lead with Ben Rimoj

Hugh Curran holds up the Tel Aviv Cup, flanked by Derek Parkin, Kenny Hibbitt, Gerry Taylor, Jim McCalliog, John McAlle, Phil Parkes and Bobby Gould. Opposite top: Jimmy Mac leads them out and (bottom) shows a caring side as Sammy Chung attends to cramp victim Gerry Taylor. Also pictured is the logo from the week-long Hapoel Games, of which Wolves' visit formed an attractive part.

Wolves remained in Israel for another four days after the game – as a reward for a successful and busy season.

They met the Mayor of Tel Aviv during their stay but were perhaps more interested in the beach time they were allowed after finishing fourth in the First Division.

As preparation for their entry into the following season's UEFA Cup, they were becoming frequent travellers, having played games in Malta and Tel Aviv and been told they would be making their usual summer trip to Scandinavia.

GREECE

Two Wolves trips to Greece, the best part of a decade apart, have each resulted in score draws.

The clash with PAOK Salonika in February, 1972, came three nights after an FA Cup fourth-round day from which the club were absent after being knocked out by Leicester but honours ended even on their travels further afield thanks to a Derek Dougan goal.

The wisdom of cramming flights and games into an already crowded schedule would be questioned today but such trips didn't seem to do Bill McGarry's squad much harm. They came home from Greece to defeat West Ham and it wasn't long before they were touching down again in foreign parts and performing magnificently against Juventus.

John Barnwell was the man in charge at Molineux when Wolves made their only repeat visit to Greece but he was nowhere to be seen on the trip.

In the wake of the club's second League Cup final triumph, he decided to stay home alone and work on his transfer policy for the summer. His main target was Peter Reid, the England under-21 and Bolton star, but several weeks of pursuit came to nothing.

Maybe the link with such names brought out a little extra in Hughie Atkinson. When the teenage midfielder flew out as part of a 14-man squad for the friendly against AEK Athens in April, 1980, he had just been named as Robinson's Midlands Player of the Month for March.

Left: Danger looming for Wolves in Greece in 1972. Phil Parkes tries to cover as Frank Munro looks on in concern.

NEW ZEALAND

Travels in a land Down Under

June 5, 1972 is a significant date in the history of Wolverhampton Wanderers – for the anoraks, at least. It was the day on which they played a game further away from Molineux than any other fixture in a history now stretching to nearly 140 years.

The match was against Wellington in New Zealand's windy city – and Bill

WELLINGTON DRUBBED BY LACK-LUSTRE WOLVES, BUT KEPT TRYING

A GLIMPSE of what it is like at the top in soccer was given by Wolverhampton Wanderers when they beat Wellington 6-0 at the Basin Reserve yesterday.

Although the winning margin of the English league first division side was convincing, the Wellington players could accept credit for a plucky performance.

The Wellington defence, especially in the first half, was the epitome of determination. The Wolverhampton strikers were kept under a tight rein for the most part in the half and it was only after the interval when Wellington adopted a more attacking attitude that the tourists were able to force openings consistently.

Weary

The play of the English team, although not unexpectedly superior to Wellington in the basics, was often not what could be expected of one of the better club teams in Europe. It bore more resemblance to that of a gifted, but very match-weary unit. Wolverhampton could have won the game by an even more convincing margin had

in fact, one of those to stand out for the home side.

C P Cameron and K R Barton had good games in the Wellington defence, with J Young and M R Jones also working hard to stymie the Wolverhampton offensives.

W Harper and I Nemet toiled well in midfield, although their distribution left something to be desired on occasions.

Bugbear

Perhaps the outstanding player for the visitors was M Bailey, a constant bugbear to Wellington as he filtered from midfield into the Wolverhampton attack with great effect

mouth for Dougan to score, from the resultant scramble.

Pressure

Although the tourists kept up the pressure with smooth, precision short passing and constantly sought to manufacture scoring situations, they could only score once more in the half, this after 40 minutes when Dougan was again on hand. There was a high cross to the goalmouth from the left side of the field, Dougan went up to beat Whiting to the ball and sent it bouncing into the net with a header.

McCalliog scored the first of his two goals after five minutes of the second half, finding the net after a goalmouth scramble.

After 55 minutes McCalliog set up Wolverhampton's fourth when he pulled the ball back off the Wellington line and sent over a low cross for Eastoe to dive and head in.

Wellington had one of their rare scoring opportunities two minutes later when S A Bruce brought into the game to replace the right wing striker, S J Boyland, three minutes earlier, scissor-kicked from the edge of the penalty area, but Parkes was in full control of the situation and made a comfortable save.

In the 76th minute Eastoe netted his second, running from the left side and beating Whiting with a fine rising shot.

The best goal of the match came three minutes later when McCalliog gained possession some 28 yards out and surprised the defence with a pile-driving shot into the top of the net.

Tribute

Wellington tried hard over the dying stages, but still without success. It is a tribute to the team's determination that they were hard on attack, even though six goals behind at the final whistle.

A bit blurry but a colour photo of Wolves in New Zealand is not to be sniffed at.....
Above: Lining up prior to the kick-off in the prestige fixture in Wellington are a clearly relaxed Dave Wagstaffe, his good mate Phil Parkes, Derek Parkin and the up-and-coming Peter Eastoe.
On the right: Mike Bailey in action.

Wellington's K R Barton comes in low between Wolverhampton Wanderers' K Hibbitt and the ball in their match at the Basin Reserve yesterday. Wolves won 6-0.

McGarry's men led 2-0 at the interval and ultimately slammed their defence-minded opponents 6-0 thanks to braces from Derek Dougan, Jim McCalliog and Peter Eastoe in a continuation of the club's entertaining goal-filled season.

Not that the manager was there to see it (see the Australia section that follows this one). This longest of long hauls was a leg too much as far as he was

WELLINGTON INVITATION XI
v.
WOLVERHAMPTON WANDERERS

BASIN RESERVE, WELLINGTON   MONDAY, JUNE 5TH. 2.30 P.M.

The Basin Reserve, where Wolves faced Wellington 43 years ago, is by no means seen mainly as a football venue. It is New Zealand's oldest Test cricket ground and was used for games in the 2015 World Cup in the summer sport. It has also hosted a rugby league Test as well as rugby union, Aussie rules fixtures and pop concerts. It was then chosen to stage a cricket game to raise money after the 2011 Canterbury earthquake that claimed 185 lives.

Right: A stamp out of a player's passport. The silver tray above is on show at Molineux and was presented to Wolves officials by the Wellington FA.

Wolves Having A Holiday In NZ?

THE English soccer team Wolverhampton Wanderers is not producing the standard of play expected of it by the New Zealand public, the New Zealand selector-coach, Mr B Truman, said after the tourists had beaten Wellington 6-0 yesterday.

"They have just finished their season at home and are fed up with travelling and soccer," he said. "The team should now be on holiday, and this is the attitude with which they are approaching their games here.

Other comments on the game were —

Mr A Muse (Wellington coach): "I am quite satisfied with the Wellington team's performance. The game was as we expected. They were much quicker thinkers."

Mr S Chung (Wolverhampton Wanderers manager-trainer): "While I must praise Wellington for their performance, it was obvious that they still need a lot more skill all around. New Zealand football

has taken a giant step over the last few years, and the introduction of the national league will help it improve more.

"Your forwards are as good as those we met at Auckland, but the Wellington links did not get back quickly enough in defence. Experience and competition is what New Zealand football needs."

Mr J Ireland (chairman of Wolverhampton Wanderers): "The Wellington team really tried and was by no means disgraced. The pitch was much better than the one on which we played Auckland on Saturday and was, in fact, better than many on which first-division football is played in England."

Elements of the Kiwi press still saw fit to suggest that the players under Sammy Chung's charge were taking their foot off the pedal a little too readily. Oh well, there is no pleasing some people, especially as Wolves won their three games in the country by 3-2, 6-0 and 2-0 margins.

Wolverhampton Wanderers F.C. Visit

A TAME LOT — THESE WOLVES

Of the overseas soccer teams to visit New Zealand, Wolverhampton Wanderers rank next to Manchester United as the most famous. Foundation members of the Football League in 1888, Wolverhampton have, all told, spent 49 seasons in the first division winning three championships and four Football Association Challenge Cups.

But the team that came here had more to offer than tradition, having made the final of the 1971/72 European Union Cup, in which 64 clubs took part.

Unlike some visiting teams, Wolverhampton brought their full League team, the only absentee being John Richards who was required for the England Under-23 team, so with three Scottish internationals (Munro, McCalliog and Curran), two Irish internationals (Dougan and Hegan) and an English international (Bailey) they had the credentials to draw bumper crowds, and this they

Auckland 2, Wolverhampton Wanderers 3
at Newmarket Park, Auckland, June 3, 1972

...and: Morris; Sibley, Latimour, Staines, R. Armstrong; Hastie, Vest, Fleet; ...ampbell, de Graaf, Davis. Subs—Turner for Vest, Thomas for de Graaf.
...rhampton: Parkes; Taylor, Parkin; Bailey, Munro, McAlle; Wagstaffe, ...cCalliog, Curran, Dougan, Hegan. Subs—Sunderland for Bailey, Hibbitt ...r Hegan.
...: Auckland—Fleet 1, Thomas 1. Wolverhampton—Dougan 2, Curran 1.
...e: Mr L. Coffman (Auckland).

---

concerned but results didn't seem to suffer from the temporary change of guard.

The handsome win over Wellington (distance from Molineux: approximately 12,000 miles) was sandwiched between more routine victories over Auckland and South Island, the latter in Christchurch, and came during an eight-game Australasian stay that spanned well under three weeks. They were called the most famous English side to visit NZ after Manchester United.

And the time in those far-away lands did not pass without a few words of criticism. Certainly, scant regard appeared to be paid to the fact Wolves had not long beaten Don Revie's Leeds in an epic title decider, contested a two-leg UEFA Cup final with Tottenham and played four games on tour on the west coast of Canada and America.

> Des Horne departed Molineux long before Wolves' 1972 visit to New Zealand but visited the country with Blackpool at the end of 1964-65. Amid shades of the Wolves-Chelsea trip to the Caribbean, the Seasiders played Sheffield United there in a series of exhibition games.

WHAT A WEEKEND!

SATURDAY, JUNE 3, 2.30

AUCKLAND PROVINCE v WOLVERHAMPTON WANDERERS

SUNDAY, JUNE 4, 1.30

AUCKLAND CITY v NEW BRIGHTON

MONDAY, JUNE 5, 2.30

BLOCKHOUSE BAY v MT. WELLINGTON

NEWMARKET PARK

20c OFFICIAL SOUVENIR PROGRAMME 20c

Not surprisingly, the 1972 adventure has been the club's only visit to New Zealand but more eyebrows may be raised at the extent of the links between there and here.

Ricki Herbert, a 1980s Molineux defender, managed the All Whites national team to their unbeaten campaign in the 2010 World Cup finals and Keith Pritchett had earlier been an assistant coach to the side, having failed to make the first-team grade with Wolves in the 1970s.

Going back even further, Freddie Goodwin was a Kiwi no 2 and in recent years Neil Emblen and Darren Bazeley have been climbing the coaching ladder there, as was Bobby Gould's son Jonathan until his return home in 2014-15.

South Island 0, Wolverhampton Wanderers 2
at English Park, Christchurch, June 7, 1972
South Island: Fleming; Davis, Griffiths. France, Park; Ferguson; Randles, Pollard, Smith; Marley, Duncan. Sub—Quirke for Duncan.
Wolverhampton: Parkes; Shaw, Parkin; Bailey, Munro, Taylor; Hegan, Sunderland, Eastoe, Curran, Wagstaffe. Subs—McCalliog for Bailey, Daley for Wagstaffe.
Goals: Wolverhampton—Eastoe 1, Munro 1.
Referee: Mr R. McDonald (Otago).

It may have taken Wolves 95 years to visit New Zealand but, in one way, their arrival was premature. They landed eight hours earlier than expected and embarrassed local officials were sent rushing from their breakfast tables by the message: 'Wolves are here'.

Wolves' players did not leave empty-handed when they flew out of a country more traditionally associated with rugby and cricket. They were each given letters, like the one addressed to John McAlle on the right, telling them there were football contracts awaiting them in their later playing years if they wished to return – plus the promise of free travel and work outside the game if required.

The match stats used on this page and the previous two represent a scoop for this publication. No other Wolves book has listed the line-ups from the three matches in New Zealand.

194 Hillsborough Road
Auckland, 4,
New Zealand.

2 June 1972

Dear John,

Welcome to New Zealand as a member of the 1972 Wolves Touring Team and welcome particularly to Auckland. I know you will enjoy your brief stay in this fine City.

The purpose of this letter is to let you know that New Zealand is always on the lookout for footballers from the U.K. We obviously cannot attract players from English or Scottish First Division football while the players are in their footballing prime. However we are very interested in players who are getting to the end of their first class careers, say at the age of 29 or 30, but who would still have some years of football left on the slower New Zealand scene.

We can arrange free passages by air to New Zealand for a player and his family and can arrange a good job and furnished or unfurnished accommodation. As you realise New Zealand football is not professional but a player, a player coach or a coach could expect expenses ranging from $10 to $40 per week.

This proposition may interest acquaintances of yours and particularly players who are considering emigrating because education facilities, job opportunities and prospects for themselves and their children here in New Zealand are so much better than in the U.K.

You have met Ken Armstrong (formerly Chelsea and England) and Tom McNab (Partick Thistle). I am sure that both of these have not regretted their decision to emigrate and continue their footballing careers on the more relaxed but still exciting New Zealand scene.

If you know of anyone who is interested just tell them to write to me at the above address and I will do the rest.

Good luck for the remainder of your tour,

D.K. Macleod
(Member, Auckland Football Association
Control Board)

The trip to lands Down Under might be something Wolves players now look back on with gratitude but serial globetrotter Jim McCalliog hoped to miss out on the opportunity of yet more travelling. In 1967, he visited Australia and New Zealand on an unofficial world tour with a Scotland squad containing Alex Ferguson and he told the excellent retro football magazine Backpass in 2007: "I had also been to Australia on a Chelsea trip when I was 18. When I heard Wolves were going there and to New Zealand, I asked Bill McGarry if I could miss it as I was a bit cheesed off with the place and wasn't a particularly good flier. But he told me it was in my contract that I had to go – then he stayed at home and his coach Sammy Chung took us!"

John Richards, having missed Wolves' 1972 trip Down Under because of an England under-23 tour, duly made it to New Zealand when he went with Steve Daley, Mel Eves and coach Brian Owen on an international B tour in May, 1978, that was managed by Bobby Robson and took in Malaysia and Singapore. Martin Patching and new Wolves signing Peter Daniel had to withdraw from the squad.

Darren Bazeley (left) and Neil Emblen, who were Wolves team-mates together in the reign of Colin Lee almost a decade and a half ago, with their wives in the years after they opted for a new life in football in New Zealand.

AUSTRALIA

Surprisingly few pictures came out of Wolves' long haul around the antipodes 43 years ago. Cine film of one or two of the fixtures has survived, though, and, thanks to exiled Wulfrunian Andy Collins, the Molineux archives are home to footage of the 3-0 victory over Western Australia in Perth.

That was the last stop-off before home on a marathon trek that also took in the games in New Zealand after Wolves had played four matches against Aberdeen in the USA and Canada.

And the tourists certainly had a bumpy landing in Oz in the shape of their opening game – a 1-0 defeat against the national XI in Victoria's state capital, Melbourne.

HIT OR MISS

Steve Corica – no worries.

Kevin Muscat – regular worries.

Zeljko Kalac – giant clanger.

Australia upsets Wolves

BY LAURIE SCHWAB

Ray Richards and Manfred Schaefer are the toast of Australian soccer after leading the national team to a 1-0 victory over Wolverhampton Wanderers at Olympic Park yesterday.

By turning back every attack Wolves launched, Richards and Schaefer gave Australia its first victory over an English first division team.

Although opposed to Irish international Derek Dougan and Scottish international Hugh Curran, it was the two brilliant Australians who looked more like world-class players.

Australia's goal was scored in the 85th minute by Attila Abonyi, after a mistake by Wolverhampton's defence.

Wolves' half-back John McAlle attempted an unwise back-pass to his goalkeeper, Philip Parkes, but Jim Rooney raced in from behind and hooked the ball to Abonyi, who faced an open goal.

The goal made Wolves the first victims of Australia's preparation for the World Cup elimination rounds in Sydney and Melbourne next year.

Wolves and Australia clash again today in Sydney and according to Wolves' coach Sammy Chung it will be a different

"Our defence, especially Richards and Schaefer, played brilliantly, but I take nothing away from the forwards, who chased the ball back into defence for the full 90 minutes."

Rasic said Victorians Billy Vojtek and Jimmy Mackay would not be playing in today's match.

They would remain in Melbourne to play for their club, Croatia, in today's State League round.

Their replacements would probably be Billy Rogers, formerly of the Melbourne club, and Terry Butler.

In yesterday's match Wolves looked nothing like a team capable of reaching the UEFA cup final.

Dougan, from whom so much has been expected, was soundly beaten by Schaefer and Richards.

Full back Derek Parkin, described by Chong as a likely member of England's World Cup squad, was inconspicuous, and Scottish international Francis Munro, was one of the few players who showed true class, was replaced at half time.

Below: Adrian Alston shoots goalwards, watched by John McAlle (left) and Jim McCalliog, as Wolves come under pressure Down Under.

MELBOURNE
AUSTRALIA

AUSTRALIA, WOLVES DRAW 2-2

By ALAN SPEERS

A blunder by Australia's Soccer captain Peter Wilson deprived the team of a momentous "double" over touring Wolverhampton Wanderers, at the Sports Ground yesterday.

Australia improved on their 1-0 defeat of Wolves in Melbourne on Sunday, but had to settle for a 2-2

apparently obsessed with the idea that Australia's defence would collapse if they poured enough high

path and the ball was in the net in a twinkling.

Rogers, 21, has been planning a trip to England

The 1972 itinerary was too much for Bill McGarry. He bailed out following the stay in America and left his trusty assistant Sammy Chung to take the strain Down Under, where physio Toby Andersen worked as unofficial no and where the side also beat South Australia 3- in Adelaide and a Queensland XI 6-2 in Brisba

While the Aussie cricketers were in England unsuccessfully trying to regain the Ashes, two matches against an Aussie National XI proved extremely taxing. The hosts ran out 1-0 winners in Melbourne and then held Wolves to a 2-2 draw in Sydney the next day in an encounter bruising enough as to have led to striker Hugh Curran being sent off for retaliation.

Wolves' summer travels in 1972 were

Top right: Adelaide's press reflects pride in how Wolves were pushed hard there. Above: The Doog on the end of a stern tackle. Opposite bottom: The city that links the club's Aussie trips of 1972 and 2009. Below: Where's a long lens when you need one? Wolves and South Australia line up.

all the more remarkable for the fact they followed a successful season that was drawn out anyway following their journey to the UEFA Cup final.

And stern task-master McGarry was determined not to ease back on the throttle. As if Australia wasn't enough after America, Canada and New Zealand, he had his players finding out their passports again a few weeks later when he took them to Sweden as part of their pre-season preparation.

Molineux's museum is well worth a visit by any Wolves fan but the foyer - home for this tray given to the club in 1972 by the Queensland FA (left) - is highly impressive, too.

WOLVES—IN LAST GAS

SA set the pace

By John Lindquist

Wolverhampton Wanderers had to call on their last reserve of physical strength and professional skill to beat South Australia in an exciting, but not classic game, at Olympic Sports Field today.

*WOLVES' Francis Munro heads for SA's goal—but the ball went over the crossbar.

● ALLAN GRISP ON TH

John Worrall left these shores around 40 years ago – just in time to see Wolves play in Melbourne and his home city of Adelaide on their 1972 trip. "It wasn't just leaving family behind that was difficult," he said of his decision to emigrate. "Being so far away from Molineux was tough as well."

WESTERN AUSTRALIA

Big smiles on Wolves' pre-season trip Down Under in 2009. No wonder....the club had just been promoted back to the Premier League under Mick McCarthy.

Thirty seven years on, it was as a build-up to a top-flight campaign that Wolves made what is so far their only return to Australia.

Mick McCarthy savoured the post-promotion 2009 trip to Perth, where his side played two games when Fulham were also in the country.

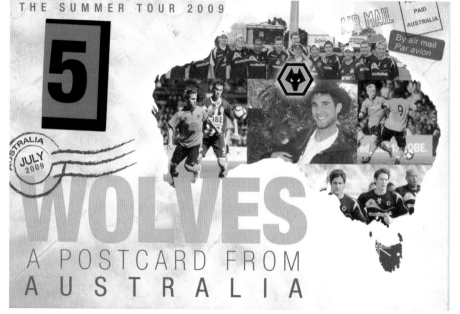

THE SUMMER TOUR 2009

5

AUSTRALIA
JULY
2009

WOLVES

A POSTCARD FROM
AUSTRALIA

Wolves used a famous Test Match cricket venue, the WACA, as their training base and members of the NSW Supporters Club (New South Wolves) were thrilled by the arrivals from England.

Among the visitors to the city during Wolves' stay was Terry Hennessey, uncle of Molineux keeper Wayne.

PORTUGAL

John McAlle was in an unusual vein of form when Wolves faced Academica Coimbra in their opening UEFA Cup assignment in September, 1971.

The defender scored only three goals in his 508 League and cup games for the club – and two of them came in the one-sided clashes with the Portuguese side; one at home, one away.

McAlle, whose other goal was in the same month in a League Cup defeat at Manchester City, shares with Derek Dougan the honour of having played more European games (18) for Wolves than anyone else. And The Doog had good reason to remember the trip to Coimbra – he scored a hat-trick on a night on which Danny Hegan was sent off for retaliation.

Both McAlle and Dougan were in the line-up when McGarry and his squad re-visited Portugal in successive seasons in the same competition in the middle of the decade.

John Richards was sent off for retaliating after scoring in the 2-0 victory in 1973-74 away to Belenenses (a club later managed by former Molineux inside-forward Jimmy Melia) but the going was altogether tougher when the side were

FEDERAÇÃO PORTUGUESA DE FUTEBOL

ACADÉMICA
WOLVERHAMPTON

BANCADA CENTRAL - 80$00

FOR HOLIDAYS AND TRAVEL

130, Widnes Road.
WIDNES. Lancs.
Tel. 051-424 5644.

EUROPEAN UNION OF FOOTBALL ASSOCIATIONS CUP.

ACADEMICA COIMBRA
V
WOLVERHAMPTON WANDERERS

Wednesday 29th September 1971.

Final details for the excursion to Portugal are as follows:
Coaches will depart from the Molineux Grounds, Waterloo Road, Wolverhampton at 07.30 hours for Birmingham Airport. Please note that the coaches will leave on time and cannot wait for any passengers arriving late.

Aircraft departs Birmingham, Elmdon Airport at 09.30 hours.

Light refreshments will be served in flight.

Arrives Oporto Airport at 11.50 hours.

Coaches will be waiting at Oporto Airport to convey you to the Hotel Bragance, Coimbra. Dinner will be served in the Hotel at 19.00 hours.

Coaches will leave the Hotel for the match at 20.15 hours.

After the match coaches will return you to the Hotel.

On Thursday morning you will leave the Hotel at 09.30 hours.

Aircraft departs Oporto Airport at 13.00 hours.

Lunch will be served in flight.

Arrives Birmingham, Elmdon Airport at 15.15 hours.

Coaches will be waiting to take you back to Wolverhampton, arriving at approximately 17.00 hours.

MATCH TICKET.

Your match ticket, the cost of which is £ 1.25., should be obtained on board the aircraft from the representative of Town's Travel Service Ltd.

JOINING AT BIRMINGHAM AIRPORT.

For those passengers who have advised us that they wish to join the tour at Birmingham Airport, you should report to the BEA Desk no later than 08.30 hours.

An author-taken photo from 1990 of the ground at Belenenses, where John Richards was sent off in 1973.

beaten 4-1 away to Porto in the first round 12 months later – a deficit they weren't quite able to retrieve in an inspired second leg.

That pairing with opponents from one of Portugal's renowned wine cities meant Wolves had opened three successive European campaigns with trips to Spain's western neighbours.

An astonishing 80,000 were present when Bert Williams played for an RAF team against a Portugal Military XI in Lisbon on February 17, 1946. Also in the side were the Stoke duo of Neil Franklin and Stanley Matthews.

Siesta time for Bill McGarry before the UEFA Cup tie away to Porto in 1974-75.

Having made their only three previous trips to Portugal in the space of three and a bit years, Wolves used consecutive summers early in the 21st century to pay their only two subsequent visits there.

It would be stretching a point to say national pride was at stake when the club did go back under the management of Dave Jones, who liked the country enough to also have taken Stockport and Cardiff there. Fitness and stamina work were the order of the day when Wolves dropped in for pre-season tours in 2001 and 2002, although the opposition was sufficiently demanding to bring about a distinctly mixed bag of results. Both trips were to the Lisbon area rather than the better known holiday trail around the Algarve. They proved difficult challenges and the visits brought a total of four defeats and a draw.

Wolves shared a dining room with Benfica at Caldas, 50 miles north of Lisbon, and visited the home of the Portuguese giants a couple of days later. The magnificent (and original) Stadium of Light was familiar to Andy Sinton – he had played there in a friendly for Tottenham.

As Wolves prepared to fly to Portugal in 2001, Maikel Aerts was due to sign from Den Bosch and Dave Jones talked excitedly of having him on board. The keeper had started training with the club but the plug was suddenly pulled on his £700,000 move and West Ham teenager Stephen Bywater was signed on loan instead in time to meet his new colleagues at Heathrow. Bywater played two of the three tour games.

Dave Jones has mixed memories of trips with Wolves to Portugal. In 2001, he ran up a big phone bill as he tried to sign Stan Collymore, who had walked out on Real Oviedo a few months earlier and announced his retirement.

A year later, the manager used the trip to the sun to get rest when he could after contracting Legionnaires' disease on holiday. Wolves' form was no sort of tonic. They crashed 5-1 against Sporting Lisbon (above) and by the only goal to John Richards's old club Maritimo just down the road in Rio Maior (below).

HIT OR MISS

Silas - failed t cut the mustard.

NORWAY

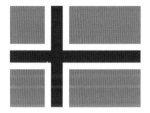

The land of fjords and mountains was an 'in' place for Wolves to travel in the second half of the 1970s.

The club were becoming much-seen visitors to Sweden but had never been to the neighbouring country to the west until Bill McGarry and his directors chose it as their destination for an end-of-season tour in 1975. Steve Kindon, in particular, made himself at home on the trip – he scored in all three of the games.

We suspect Wolves players and the supporters who have trailed them round these parts will have memories of hot days, long, light nights – and more than a few mosquitoes, especially in the more northerly regions. So this photo and the ones over the page may spark some recollections of an altogether different weather pattern.....

Steve Kindon splashes his way through to score one of his two goals in the rain-sodden 3-1 win over Alesund in May, 1975. The forward's long-time big pal John Richards is seen in the background but the side's other goal came from left-winger John Farley.

Making a claim to being Norway's raining champions

Wolves were a considerable way north on Norway's unusual west coast when they flew out for a three-match end-of-season tour in May, 1975.

Having finished 12th in the top flight, they found goals easy to come by during their travels as they preceded this soggy victory against Alesund by winning 1-0 against Mjondalen and 8-1 over Odds Ballklubb in Skien, with John Richards hitting a hat-trick.

Two months later, the squad were back in Scandinavia for five games in Sweden.

Above: Kenny Hibbitt shoots for goal, with Mike Bailey looking on. Left: Derek Parkin aqua-planes into a tackle as John McAlle also splashes his way into the deep end. On the opposite page, bottom, Wolves show their appreciation to the crowd before kick-off against Odds in Skien.

Bobby Gould, an FA Cup winner with West Ham just before, bumped into Wolves' squad in Alesund in 1975 when over there with West Ham.

But the sun came out, too

Da Rune André trakk i Wolverhampton-trøya

Det var et stort øyeblikk for «mini-Wolves», Rune André Killingstad, da han meget stolt

godt foran mandagens oppgjør mot Rosenborg på Lerkendal. – Det var derfor synd at bare

84-åring slått ned og ranet i sitt hjem

Det eneste den 84 år gamle mannen fra Ådal kan huske fra det som skjedde med ham tirsdag kveld, er at det plutselig sto en yngre kar ved siden av sengen hans og sa: «Hit med pengan!» Klokken var

Mike Bailey meets his Mjondalen counterpart and a young admirer (top far left) while match-winner Steve Kindon causes more havoc above. Below: Time for some sightseeing that took the Wolves squad's breath away.....

Are we really flying on this?

Wolves were back in Norway in 1977, this time with Sammy Chung in charge, when the town of Skien was on their match-day itinerary for a second successive visit.

You might have thought that winning the Division Two title over a 42-game season and playing six ties in the major cups to boot was a full year's work. But Wolves' players were then asked to play three mid-May tour games on successive nights – all of which were won by convincing margins (4-2, 5-0 and 6-0).

HIT OR MISS

Haavard Flo – only a modest flo of goals.

Steffen Iversen – a fleeting impact in the Premier League first time round.

Gunnar Halle – nor way will he go down as a great.

Right: John Richards' cap honouring his England under-21 duty against Norway in Bergen that came only a few days after he was in the country on Wolves' tour. Above: Secretary Phil Shaw (with raincoat over his left arm) and Sammy Chung (far right) take a last look back as they step aboard for a short internal flight on the sort of ageing plane on which they probably wouldn't have wanted to travel that much further!

vikingwolves

Norman Bell and Billy Rafferty lead the charge against Kolbotn, where Steve Daley was skipper. Opposite: Press coverage of Grand v Wolves.

The going was harder when Wolves returned to Norway in May, 1978, by which time Sammy Chung had been replaced by John Barnwell.

Just before leaving for home, the side lost to Molde, who became one of Norway's finest clubs.

But, as is usual for trips to those parts, there was also some shooting practice, with both Ski-Kolbotn and Grand put to the sword to the tune of four goals.

The first of those games was in Oslo and saw a goal by John Black, who then netted twice against Grand.

Den helt store festforestillingen ble det ikke da Wolverhampton i går kveld gjestet Bodø og Grand. Bodø-guttene spilte seg til et hederlig resultat og publikum fikk se fem scoringer. Likevel — det helt store spillet som man kanskje har lov til å forvente av feterte proffer som Wolves, det uteble.

Noe av forklaringen på at engelskmennene ikke fikk briljere så stort, ligger nok i Grand-guttenes innsats — først og fremst før pause. Respektløst tok de kampen opp og klarte å holde nullen til 10 minutter ut i 2. omgang.

Da var det også stort sett slutt — både med kreftene og marke-ringene i Grands midtforsvar. I løpet av fem minutter laget innbytteren John Black det nokså svart for Grand-gutte med to scoringer.

1. DIVISJON

Lillestr. —Bodø.Glimt	2—0	
Molde —Lyn	1—3	
Moss —Start	0—2	
Steinkjer —Bryne	1—2	
Viking —Vålerengen	tirsdag.	

Start	5	4	1	0	9- 3	9
Bryne	5	3	1	1	9- 4	7
Lillestrøm	5	3	1	1	9- 5	7
Viking	4	2	2	0	6- 2	6
Vålerengen	4	2	1	1	8- 4	5

Grands Arne Inge Svendsen (t.v.) hadde mange harde dueller mot Wolverhamptons forsvars-... Wolves-manageren Sammy Chung hadde for øvrig mange lovord å si om

Viking Wolves are not shy in showing their love for the players who first attracted them. Although they now have solid roots in Bergen, one of their favoured watering holes, the Bohemen in Oslo, has had pictures of Kenny Hibbitt, John Richards and Dave Wagstaffe on inside walls that are a shrine to English football.

It was in Oslo that Graham Taylor was famously and unflatteringly captured on the touchline by a TV documentary in his time as an international manager but Wolves didn't go back to Norway until the final months of Dave Jones' reign in the summer of 2004.

A squad just relegated from the Premier League were based some 250 miles north of the Arctic Circle in Tromso, from where some of their players avoided a three-hour coach journey by being transported to the opening game in Nordreisa by a small Piper aircraft – and then returning to their hotel by boat. Even the nervous fliers among the party must have recovered sufficiently because Wolves won 3-2 but they followed up with defeats in their other two matches, the second of them against Lyn Oslo in the Ullevaal Stadium – the same arena in which a Norwegian commentator had gone off at a colourful, never-to-be-forgotten tangent in the 1980s to describe how our boys had taken 'a hell of a beating.'

It was much quieter 11 years ago at the Ullevaal, as can be seen right. The photo, like the closest banner, is supplied by Berlin Wolves.

GIBRALTAR

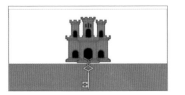

Wolves had just been relegated when they visited Gibraltar for the four-team Rock Cup in 1976 – a trip that gave them the chance to score some psychological points over two of the sides they would face in the following season's Second Division. And it was an opportunity they grabbed with both hands by defeating Blackburn 3-2 and then running out 4-1 victors in the final against Sheffield United. The games, both staged in late May, are unrecorded in Wolves' record books, so, again, we are happy to provide some extra 'flesh' on the bones of this stay in the tiny British territory.

Sammy Chung's men roared into a three-goal first-half lead against Blackburn thanks to efforts by Gerry O'Hara (2) and Steve Kindon but then rode their luck with their opponents not only pulling two back late on but also hitting the woodwork three times. With Kenny Hibbitt out because of a groin strain, Colin Brazier played his first senior match for the club in this team: Pierce, Sunderland, Palmer, Daley, Bailey, Brazier, O'Hara, Carr, Kindon, Patching, Farley (Bell, 45).

The victory over Jimmy Sirrel's Blades on May 27 was more emphatic, thanks largely to another storming start. Wolves were four up at half-time against one of the clubs with whom they had just taken the drop, Kindon (2), Geoff Palmer and Willie Carr (penalty) netting. United's consolation in front of a 5,500 crowd came late on from Paul Garner. Wolves team: Pierce, Sunderland, Palmer, Daley, Bailey, Brazier, Carr, O'Hara, Kindon (Bell), Patching, Farley (Hibbitt).

Kindon was named the player of the tournament and skipper Bailey received from the territory's Governor the winners' spoils – a trophy based on a model of the imposing rock. Wolves' side are seen below in a Gibraltar Chronicle photo with a predictable background, one or two of their group still sporting tracksuits forever connected to the 1974 League Cup final. There was an unhappy sequel, though, to a competition in which Graham Taylor's Lincoln also took part. Norman Bell suffered a suspected fractured arm in a fall on the shale pitch.

The programme for the tournament, shown right, went at the time for a mere two shillings but has been seen on sale on ebay recently for £200. So, if you went and still have your souvenir, cherish it!

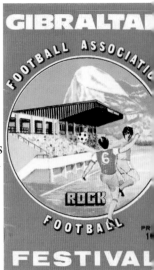

VICTORIA STADIUM

Wolves were the busiest of Bs when they ventured back to the Rock in 1992. This time they beat a Gibraltar XI 5-2 with goals by Mark Burke (2), Steve Bull, Tom Bennett and Paul Birch.

The Monday evening fixture in January was arranged because of the club's absence from FA Cup fourth-round weekend following a plucky defeat at Nottingham Forest and came during a run of five successive League victories in which Bully was predictably well to the fore.

The record-breaking striker, not surprisingly, was the main hero of Robert 'Poppy' Perez, who has lived on the Rock all his life and was then serving there in the Royal Gibraltar Regiment of the British Army. The two men are pictured above, with evidence also captured of secretary Keith Pearson's attendance on the winter break.

WITH THIS ROCK, I THEE WED
Bertie Lutton dropped in on Gibraltar when he made one of his 21st century visits back to Europe from his long-time home in Australia. His Wolverhampton-based son Lee was married there in the summer of 2010.

The Gibraltar Chronicle joined Wolves' entourage on a sight-seeing tour the following day, reporter Clara Quantrill writing: "Most of the (extremely fit) team looked slightly daunted at the idea of climbing the rock. They were only satisfied when told there was a cable car up – and a pub at the top."

187

KUWAIT

KUWAIT TIMES, WEDNESDAY FEB. 22, 1984

Kuwait hold Wolves 0-0

SOCCER

By MOHAMMED ATTASI

ONE of the Kuwait National Soccer Team selections held

In the second half, Kuwait adopted 4-3-3 tactics and managed to present some effective attacks. Yet they failed miserably in finding the target. In fact the local squad

Above and left: A cutting from the Kuwait Times shows John Burridge on his toes as John Pender stretches.

Sami Al Jaber's arrival at Molineux in 2000 caused great interest in the Gulf and looked likely to lead Wolves back to the region. Two games in Saudi Arabia were arranged, for separate visits, but the striker was not a major success in the Championship and, as his star fell, the matches in Jeddah and Riyadh were scrapped.

Manager Graham Hawkins was thankful that what he called 'cool, windy conditions' greeted his Wolves players on an unusual two-match trip to the Gulf 31 years ago. It is a recollection with which Mel Eves begs to disagree. "It's okay for the gaffer to say that – he wasn't playing!" he said. "I remember it as being warm; humid as well – enough to tell me that the players will have a tough time if the World Cup goes to Qatar."

Wolves were in a hopeless survival battle when they flew east in the second half of February, 1984, to face opponents who were warming up for qualifying games for the 1986 Mexico World Cup.

Against the background of a failed attempt to sign teenage Southampton striker Ian Baird on loan, they showed why their attacking resources were in need of strengthening as they ground out two 0-0 draws with the Kuwait national side 48 hours apart.

Wolves included apprentice centre-half Graham Rodger and untried Tim Flowers in a 17-man

squad but, for the first game, kept the side who had just drawn at home to Manchester United.

Flowers, Geoff Palmer, Dale Rudge, Rodger and David Wintersgill were called up for the second match, so only John Humphrey did not get a full game on the trip. The photo below, from the Al-Qabas newspaper, shows Wayne Clarke ready in waiting for a chance.

Hawkins, who had embraced the adventure as a welcome change of scenery, was interested to observe the opulence on the streets. "Money is no object here," he told the Express & Star. "If the Kuwaitis want something, they just go out and buy it." The paper also reported that the streets were full of Mercedes, with even amateur players turning up for training in gleaming Limousines.

It would be too simplistic to say Wolves' 4-0 defeat at Aston Villa immediately after their return home was a result of too much travel and too much exertion. They lost most weeks in that season's top flight.

They certainly can't claim they were hung-over. The Gulf state was 'dry' and Eves added: "Not having alcohol didn't bother me but one or two of the lads may have been a bit thirsty."

حمد درويش يبعد الكرة من امام مهاجم انكليزي وعماد رفا

MISCELLANEOUS

We round off this publication about Wolves' long and varied history of travel with some photos that we were not able to place specifically with any certainty.

The picture on the left, which shows a group of players led by Kenny Hibbitt and John Holsgrove, may not be in the sharpest of focus but we believe it was taken at the end of 1969-70.....either on the three-match tour to Yugoslavia or the excursion to Italy that

followed it. If it were the latter trip, this game would be the one against Forte del Marmi that is not mentioned in any of the record books about the club.

Wolves were in the country for two Anglo Italian Cup fixtures and, with little time for laundry matters, it is entirely plausible they might have worn their change strip even against a team whose colours did not clash with their gold and black.

We mulled long and hard over the setting for this large colour photo right and sufficient doubt remained for us to defer from using it in the country-by-country sections earlier.

But we now believe it was taken on the club's end-of-season tour as champions early in the summer of 1958, possibly against Zurich Grasshoppers.

While we are in a 'where was this taken?' frame of mind, we have great pleasure in showing this shot of the late and popular former Wolves chairman John Ireland, who was responsible for some of the photos in this book.

A nice sun-filled pavement cafe could be in any number of places and the fact he was such a regular companion to the team keeps it as a wide choice of possible venues.

Who knows where this relaxed beach shot might have been taken? It's very difficult to say but the hairstyles of the likes of John Richards, John Holsgrove, Phil Parkes and Mike Bailey point us towards the early to mid-1970s, so maybe Yugoslavia or Italy, America even? We know the location of the final photograph in this book....it's a cruise out of Vancouver in 1963, fully enjoyed by Jimmy Murray (left) and Freddie Goodwin.